Mastering Fine Decorative
PAINT
TECHNIQUES

W. EUGENE SMITH

CRE▲TIVE
HOMEOWNER®

Mastering Fine Decorative

PAINT
TECHNIQUES

SHARON ROSS
AND ELISE KINKEAD

CREATIVE HOMEOWNER®, Upper Saddle River, New Jersey

Editorial Director: Timothy O. Bakke
Art Director: W. David Houser
Production Manager: Ann Bernstein

Senior Editor: Kathie Robitz
Assistant Editor: Paul Rieder
Copyeditor: Louise I. Driben
Proofreaders: Craig Clark, Laura DeFerrari

Design and Layout: Glee Barre
Project Photography: Don Wong
Interior Photography (except where noted): Mark Samu
Additional Photography: Phillip Ennis (page 31, design by
    Gail Whiting); Steve Gross and Susan Daley (page 28);
    George Mattei (page 27); John Parsekian (pages 48–53,
    57, 69, 114–115, 118 [right], 119); courtesy of Zinsser
    (page 91)
Faux Finishes (except where noted): Lucianna Samu
Additional Faux Finishes: Silver and chocolate faux finish by
    John Agnese and Frank Carballeira Decorative Art and
    Design (page 30); faux finish and mural "Cave Painting"
    by John Agnese and Frank Carballeira Decorative Art and
    Design (pages 66-67)
Cover Design: Glee Barre
Cover Photography: Don Wong

Manufactured in the United States of America

Current Printing (last digit)
10   9

Mastering Fine Decorative Paint Techniques
Library of Congress Catalog Card Number: 98-89443
ISBN: 1-58011-064-9

CREATIVE HOMEOWNER®
A Division of Federal Marketing Corp.
24 Park Way
Upper Saddle River, NJ 07458
www.creativehomeowner.com

Dedication

To everyone who seeks a home that has individuality and personality, and to the skilled artisans who help them achieve it through the use of harmonious color and texture.

Acknowledgments

We wish to thank the many people who helped make this book possible. Among them Shelley O'Brien, Elise Kinkead's assistant; Don Wong, photographer; David Wlaschin, Don Wong's assistant; the National Decorating Products Association; Steve Sides, National Paint and Coating Association; the Paint Quality Institute; Kenneth Charbonneau, consultant, color marketing, Benjamin Moore & Company; Carol Benysek and Bonnie Rohow at Abbott Paint & Carpet, St. Paul, MN; Eleanor McGough, Lathrop Paint Supply Co., Minneapolis, MN; and the staff at Wet Paint, Inc., St. Paul, MN.

CONTENTS

INTRODUCTION

The past twenty years have seen an explosion of interest in the art of decorative painting. In the search for ways to create homes with individuality and personality, homeowners, interior designers, and architects alike have rediscovered the beauty of the classic faux finishes. With these centuries-old techniques, they have found a practical tool for adding texture, detail, mystical color, illusion, drama, and much more than is

possible with plain paint. It's no wonder the interest in these fine decorative finishes shows no signs of abating. If you are looking for an exciting, highly personal way to decorate, mastering one or more of these techniques will give you the effect that you seek.

At first glance, these methods may look difficult because they appear to be exacting. Some are, but most are not. All require time, energy, commitment, and the willingness to put up with some mess. It's true, the techniques also call for a little study, careful planning, and some thoughtful attention to the overall project. But you do not have to be an accomplished artist to render them. Your sincere effort is more important to your success than any outright skill. You can learn—and practice—as you go along, and *Mastering Fine Decorative Paint Techniques* will help you do just that.

This book takes you step-by-step through the most popular decorative finishing techniques, starting with sponging, probably the simplest, and ending with wood graining, one of the more difficult but most beautiful decorative finishes. Each procedure is grouped with similar styles of decorative painting, but each is explained completely, even as it builds on the previous methods in that style. Each group, in turn, builds on previous ones. For example, the technique Sponging on with Two Colors builds on skills that you will learn from Sponging on with One Color; the ragging techniques, which are slightly more difficult, use a stroke basic to sponging. Numerous cross-references help you go back to quickly review such pertinent information. As you work your way through the techniques, you will build ever-increasing skill and confidence.

Throughout the book, the emphasis is on the method, not the finished room setting. A final photo shows you how the completed finish looks so you have a frame of reference for your work. However, a generous sprinkling of photographs of finished rooms throughout the book demonstrates how effective these techniques prove to be in decorating a home.

In addition, the text accompanying each technique contains a wealth of practical information about products, as well as some tricks, tips, and cautions to help you achieve success. As for their color schemes, they are simply suggestions rendered for photographic purposes. You can develop your own successful ones: That's a big part of the fun of the faux finishes. Most techniques give you guidance as to what kinds of color combinations work best.

All this is intended to inspire your creativity and to give you the courage to try something new. Don't worry if the outcome is less than perfect. These are fantasy finishes. As such, they are quite charming even if they have a folk-art, less-than-perfect look.

Before the step-by-step instructions begin, you'll find five chapters of solid technical information about color, paint, glazes, brushes, tools, repairing surfaces, and mixing your own paints and glazes.

Although this book is geared to beginners, experienced decorative painters will find it helpful in moving beyond the basics. And remember, the real goal is developing interiors that go well beyond the ordinary.

The Colorful History of
Decorative Painted Finishes

Humans seem to have an inborn and irresistible urge to use paint to decorate the surfaces around them. Examples date back into antiquity. Prehistoric humans did it on the walls of their caves. The ancient Egyptians did it on the walls inside their pyramids. The ancient Romans did it on the walls in their villas, and long before them, the Mycenaeans living on Crete did it on the walls of their homes and on their pottery. In

fact, Mycenaean pottery known to be 4,000 years old has the earliest known examples of faux marble. So the decorative finishes are ancient and honorable art forms, but that doesn't explain the present-day revival of their popularity. Why now?

The answer probably is threefold. It's a bold counter-reaction to the plainness of mid-twentieth century interior design; it reflects a growing appreciation for things, especially houses, that reflect life in a gentler, kinder, more refined age; and it certainly signifies a growing appreciation for the uniqueness and individuality of handcrafted items in an age dominated by machine-made, mass-produced, mass-marketed goods.

The truth is, decorative finishes have cycled in and out of favor throughout history. Each time they resurface, it's for a combination of aesthetic and practical reasons.

Marbling

During the Renaissance, for example, there was plenty of exquisite marble available, but painted versions became highly fashionable anyway. The ability to render realistic marbles rose to the level of a high art. Beginning in the thirteenth century, painted marble was used in place of real marble in churches for two reasons: It was less expensive, and the load-bearing walls and columns weren't strong enough to bear the weight of stone. Besides, it was challenging to paint something so realistic that it was difficult to distinguish it from the real thing.

The popularity of marbling continued through the Baroque period; then it quietly faded away for several centuries. It revived with the discovery of Pompeii in the mid-eighteenth century. The powerful impact this archaeological excavation had on Western art and politics can't be understated. It sparked the intense interest in classical antiquity that gave rise to the neoclassical movement in architecture and all the decorative arts, and the revival of the democratic republic form of government.

By the late eighteenth century, furniture design and interior design were solidifying into art forms. Robert Adams, the great English architect, was largely responsible for integrating architecture and furnishings using neoclassical themes. All over Europe and America, interest in and appreciation of marbling, called *faux marbre*, and painted wood graining, called *faux bois*, remained strong well into the nineteenth century.

The demand for both techniques remained especially strong in the early eighteenth century during the simultaneous French Empire, English Regency, and American Federalist periods. This popularity reflected the influence of classicism, but it also reflected the realities of the Napoleonic Wars. A combination of trade blockades and a shortage of ships meant beautiful materials, such as marble and exotic woods, were almost impossible to obtain. Certainly, that was part of the reason Dolly Madison and her architect, Benjamin Latrobe, decided to use marbling on the walls of the oval drawing room when they decorated the White House in 1811. It's too bad the British had the audacity to try and burn it down in 1814.

Wood Graining

Painting surfaces to resemble wood dates just as far back as painting them to look like marble. From time immemorial, one method of wood graining or another has been used to give ordinary woods and non wooden surfaces the appearance of some exotic species. However, its popularity was not as persistent as that of marbling, except in cultures such as ancient Egypt where wood was rare. (How rare? Well, the capitals atop classical columns have curved volutes—scroll-like spirals—because they imitate Egyptian columns, which were made of bundles of papyrus reeds instead of wood or stone. The tops of the reeds curled under the weight of the lintels and a classical motif was born.)

As a decorative finish, wood graining has had its role to play from time to time in European history, but it always has been popular in the United States. If fact, here it has been more popular than marbling, which probably reflects America's long-standing love affair with wood.

The wood-graining techniques became established as an art form in the nineteenth century with the development of the technology that made it possible to make furniture with wood veneers. It became popular to use tropical woods such as mahogany for veneers. These woods were as rare and as expensive as they were coveted, and that gave rise to the fashion of imitating them with paint. The techniques quickly gained popularity in England and, naturally, here in America.

Actually, painting pine furniture to make it look like more desirable wood had been an American folk-art form from the very beginning, brought here by English, Dutch, German, and Scandinavian settlers. Some of the graining was primitive, but it has a naive charm that is still appreciated today.

Glazing

Glazing surfaces has a similar ancient past. In the twelfth century, Italian artists used glazes made with nut oils and varnishes. In the early Renaissance they applied glazes of yellow oil and varnish over tin to simulate gold.

Just as the excavation at Pompeii influenced art, so did the opening of the Orient in the late seventeenth century. The discovery of Oriental lacquerware, with its highly polished surfaces, led to imitations made with paint, tinted shellac, and varnish.

By the late nineteenth century, most house painters had the ability to produce wood graining, glazing, and marbling for their clients. Sometimes they created these finishes by hand, other times by mechanical means. Their skills carried on into the stenciled borders popular in the Arts and Crafts, Art Nouveau, and Art Deco movements. By the late 1920s, influenced by the Bauhaus movement in Germany, modernism began to spin out of the Art Deco movement and minimalism took over. Ornamentation fell into disfavor as interior design emphasized spare structural forms with white-on-white walls. The International style was born.

The privation of the Depression and the material scarcities of World War II prevented any counter-movements to the asceticism of the International style for nearly 20 years. After World War II, the tremendous shortage of housing forced attention on building as many houses as quickly and cheaply as possible. In the process, all suggestions of decoration were abandoned as being too costly and, therefore, unnecessary. It took more than 30 years—until the late 1970s—for people to rediscover the charm, practicality, and durability of decorative finishes. As people restored old houses and built new houses in older styles, they found that these finishes were essential to their decorating plans. As their interest in the classic paint finishes blossomed, manufacturers responded with a host of helpful products. This interest has lasted long enough now that one thing is certain: It isn't a flash in the pan. Decorative finishes are here to stay.

PART I

Technical Information

Subtle but vital color lies at the heart of every fine decorative paint technique; it's the key to every successful project. That's why any discussion of the techniques must begin with the aspect of color. The prospect of using color as a creative tool is exciting, but it also presents a challenge: making choices about the right ones for your project. What look you select will depend on a given technique, how well one color harmonizes with the others in a room, and how successfully they complement a room's style and function.

The Magic of Color

Because the human eye can distinguish 10 million variations in color, narrowing down your choices to just a few may feel daunting. However, you don't have to be paralyzed by the prospect of this abundance. Let the following review of the basics of color get you started.

*The **apricot color** of the walls in this dining room is an excellent choice where food is served and people socialize. Its warmth balances nicely with the cool green used in the next room.*

Three different colors *applied in a harlequin pattern put a unique spin on this folding screen.*

This chapter outlines the accepted principles of color's use in interior design, shows you how it works in terms of perception, guides you in developing color schemes, and explains how to use color with confidence.

From the beginning, it's important to understand three basic truths:

- Color is complex
- Color preferences are intensely personal
- No one color stands alone; it needs others to reinforce and modify it. In other words, it belongs in the context of a complete overall scheme

In fact, it is the color scheme, the artful harmonizing of hues with their surroundings, that gives color its magical ability to delight and fool the eye, affect emotion, inspire the psyche, and satisfy the soul—all at the same time.

What is Color?

Each color can be described by three qualities: *hue* (which is another name for color and is used to indicate the family to which a specific color belongs), *value*, and *intensity*. The way these characteristics are combined in a given color determines its specific identity. While all three traits are of equal importance, obviously value and intensity cannot exist without hue. This makes hue the first among equals. It's also the easiest to understand because it's the principle behind the organization of the color wheel, a visual device that shows you how colors are derived and how they influence one another. (See the illustration below.)

The Color Wheel

You think you see color. However, scientifically speaking, what you really see is light that's reflected by an object, whether that object is a bouquet of flowers, a dress, or a painted wall. Light is visible electromagnetic radiation (energy) that travels in wavelengths from an object to your eyes. Your optic nerves change these light waves into electrochemical signals that create a specific color image in your brain. Because light waves are of different lengths, with each wavelength creating a specific color image, the exact color you see depends on the number and length of the light waves reflected off the object. Paint contains a substance called pigment, which reflects light waves of varying lengths, thus creating its color.

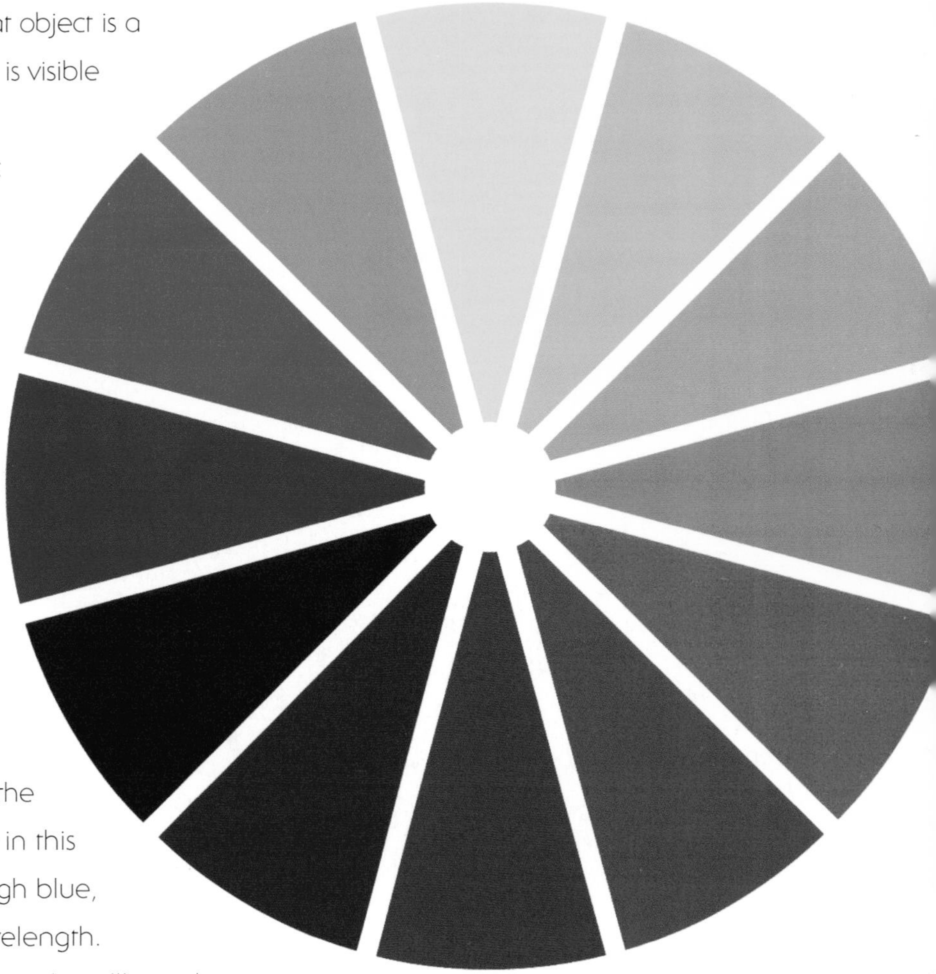

Sunlight is the purest form of light. As it passes through a prism, its wavelengths bend at different angles and break into a rainbow-like band called the visible spectrum. All the pure or true colors appear in this band—from violet, the shortest wavelength, through blue, green, yellow, and orange to red, the longest wavelength. Colors always appear in this order. Study this band, and you'll see that although each color is distinct, each one flows out of and into the colors on either side of it until 12 colors are clearly visible. These 12 colors constitute the color wheel. To make them easier to understand, experts divide colors into three groups: primary, secondary, and intermediate.

The Color Wheel

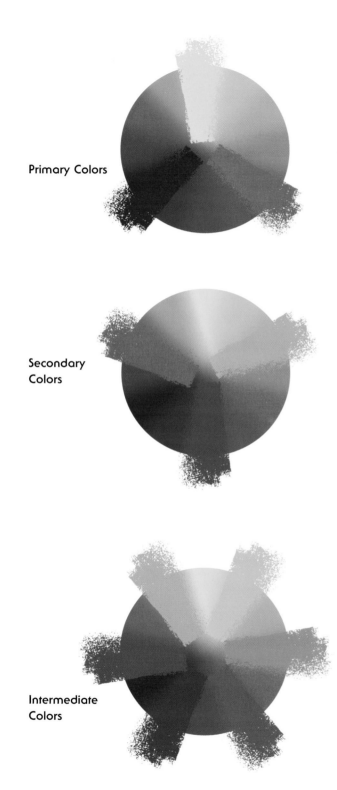

Primary Colors

Secondary Colors

Intermediate Colors

The three primary colors—red, yellow, and blue—are called primary because they are the ones that, in painting, are not broken down into other colors but are used to mix all the others. The dictionary refers to them as "psychological primaries," because this paint-mixing system and its color wheel are really just an arbitrary construct: For example, the primary color red in this book is printed from the process "subtractive primaries" of magenta, yellow, and cyan (a pale blue), with the addition of black. However, for the purposes of paint mixing, the primaries should be considered a given. In this system, these three colors lie equal distances apart on the color wheel, with all of the other colors between them.

The three secondary colors—orange, green, and violet—are obtained by combining equal amounts of two primary colors. Red and yellow make orange; yellow and blue make green; blue and red make violet. Each secondary color lies halfway between its two primaries.

The six intermediate colors—red-orange, yellow-orange, yellow-green, blue-green, blue-violet, and red-violet—bridge the gaps between the primary and secondary colors. Each intermediate color is made by combining one primary color with one secondary color. Yellow combined with green, for example, makes yellow-green.

These 12 colors form the basic color wheel. There are no absolute rules about how to use them, but their positions on the wheel produce natural color combinations that always work well together. The following are the five most common combinations of colors:

Complementary colors. Colors located directly across the color wheel from one another balance each other when used together. Red and green are complements. So are blue-green and red-orange. Note that any single set of complementary colors contains all the primary colors. Complementary colors neutralize one another when mixed, producing a dull, flat gray.

Complementary
Colors

Analogous colors. These are any three colors lying next to one another on the color wheel. Yellow-orange, yellow, and yellow-green are analogous colors.

Analogous
Colors

Triad colors. Any three colors set equal distances apart on the color wheel are triad colors. Red, yellow, and blue, for example, make a triad.

Triad Colors

Split complementary. This is defined as a color joined by the colors on each side of its complement. Blue-green, the complement of which is red-orange, forms a split-complementary scheme when used with orange and red.

Split-complementary
Colors

Double-split complementary. This scheme involves four colors, one from each side of two complementary colors. Yellow-green and yellow-orange, located on each side of yellow, form a double-split complementary scheme when mated with red-violet and blue-violet, located on each side of violet, yellow's complement.

Double-split
Complementary
Colors

Expanded Colors

Those 12 pure hues and their natural harmonies are but a hint, the barest whisper, of the colors that are available to you. Two additional color groups are needed to flesh out the basic color wheel: complex colors and neutral colors.

Complex Colors. These are the third- and fourth-tier colors that result from making two additional types of combinations. Blend two secondary colors, and you'll get a tertiary color. Purple and orange, for example, produce a rich brown with purple undertones. Combine two tertiary colors, and you'll produce a quaternary color. While less vibrant, these complex colors are richer and subtler than pure hues.

Neutral Colors. These include the three classics: white, black, and gray. Technically, white and black are noncolors because they either reflect or absorb all the light waves in the visible spectrum, producing white or black, respectively. Pure grays result from mixing white and black in varying proportions.

Value and Intensity

Now color's two other characteristics come into play. You've probably noticed that pure hues are seldom used in interior design, at least not together and not in large areas. That's because they're too strong. Instead, these colors are modified to make them less intense, more sophisticated and harmonious. It's this opportunity to vary hues both up and

Neutral off-white plays against the intensity of citrus green on this checkered wall.

down the palette that results in the incredible variety of colors. However, it's important to understand that these modifications do not change the colors' basic relationships to one another. In fact, they enhance them by working together quietly to give you the control required to develop the contrast that is fundamental to a successful color scheme.

Value

This is a color's lightness or darkness. You can control a value by adding white, black, or gray to a pure hue. Add white, and it becomes a *tint*. The more white, the lighter and paler the tint. Very light colors are called *pastels*. Add black, and the color becomes a *shade*. The more black, the darker the shade. Add gray, and the color becomes a *tone*.

On the color wheel, tints lie inside the pure hues and move toward the center as they become lighter; shades lie outside the pure hues and move toward the perimeter as they become darker.

To judge a specific color's value, compare it with a neutral gray scale. This scale is a vertical bar divided into 11 sections that range from pure white to complete black. In between lie progressively darker shades of gray in 10-percent increments, with middle gray at the center: All colors at the same level on the bar have the same value. This neutral gray scale is used by the machines that analyze a fabric's color so that paint stores can custom-mix a color to match it, for example.

No matter what the color, different values create different moods in a room. All tints, including pale neutrals, produce a soft, light, airy look. This makes them popular choices in

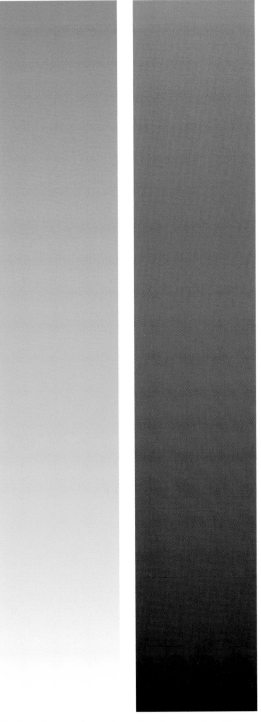

Each color *on the color wheel can mix with white into progressively lighter tints, left, or with black into a range of darker shades, right.*

Deeper colors *are typically used on accessories, although they can look sophisticated on walls.*

interior design. Dark colors produce a controlled, dignified, and cosmopolitan ambiance: For example, burgundy and dark green are the most popular color choices among the affluent. However, while these colors work well in sophisticated settings, their very darkness makes them best used as accents in most rooms. Bright colors—those close to pure hues—impart an energetic, contemporary exuberance that is so stimulating it can

be overwhelming. This is especially true when two or more of
them are used together. For this reason bright colors are often
reserved for use in active spaces, such as a child's bedroom or
a playroom, or as accents in a room. When applied over large
areas, their impact can be subdued if they are surrounded with
plenty of white-painted surfaces.

Intensity

Intensity, also called *chroma*, describes a color's brightness
(sometimes called *purity*) or dullness (sometimes called
saturation) without regard to its actual tint or shade. In other
words, a dark color can be bright or dull, as can a light color.

To increase a color's brightness, add more of the pure hue. The
more the pure hue dominates, the more vivid and intense the
resulting color. There are three ways to decrease a color's
intensity. In order of preference, they are

- Adding its complementary hue in the same value
- Adding a native color equivalent to its complement
- Adding black

The native colors—yellow ochre, raw sienna, burnt sienna,
raw umber, burnt umber, and lampblack—are the basic
inorganic pigments used in artist's oil paints. They have their
origins in powders ground from naturally pigmented earth, colored by minerals (mainly
iron oxides)—except lampblack, which is almost pure carbon. Each one complements a
pure hue and can be used to dull or lessen the intensity of the color and its natural
complement. Yellow ochre, for example, is a medium, dull yellow that blunts the
intensity of other colors, especially other yellows, greens, and purples, its natural
complement. The more native color added to a pure hue, the grayer and duller the
result. To get the best result, ask for advice at a reputable paint or artist's supply store
about what native color you need to create your specific hue.

When selecting a hue, *remember that value,
which is the lightness or darkness of a color,
affects the mood of a room. All tints, including
pale neutrals, produce a soft, light, and airy
feeling, for example.*

Color's Physical and Emotional Effects

Color's power lies in its ability to influence whatever it surrounds, including the mood of every person in the room. It arises from both visual temperature and emotional quotient, each caused by the length of the color's light waves.

Visual Temperature

All colors have a temperature—either warm or cool. *Warm colors* contain red or yellow, and range from red-violet through yellow-green. They are stimulating and inviting because their long light waves advance toward you, making them seem closer than they actually are. That's why they make a room seem smaller.

Pale green walls *evoke a cool, refreshing feeling in this room.*

Cool colors contain blue, and range from green through violet, although the term cool is also used to describe the three neutrals—white, black, and gray. Because of their shorter light waves, cool colors appear to recede, creating a fresh, calm, unrestricted feeling that helps make a room feel larger.

Scientific color tests prove that color affects temperature sensations. In these tests, occupants rated a warm-colored room as feeling warmer than rooms painted white or other cool colors, even though the rooms themselves were the same temperature. Similar tests showed that occupants in a blue or gray west-facing room felt measurably cooler on a hot afternoon than those in a warm-colored west-facing room—even though, again, the room temperatures were the same.

Emotional Quotient

Emotional quotient describes color's ability to produce emotional reactions in people. Think about how you use color-related terms to describe various emotions. For instance, consider such common expressions as being green with envy, rosy with optimism, blue with sadness, red with anger, and black with rage. Also, think about color's emotion-inducing capacity when developing your overall scheme. Ideally, you'll want your colors to create a suitable ambiance for your room because they feel, as well as look, right.

Red. Red has the longest wavelength of all the colors in the visible spectrum. That means it advances toward you, which makes it bold, energetic, and warm. The scientific color tests mentioned on the previous page showed that pure red, which lies closest on the visible spectrum to infrared, can increase the heartbeat and raise body temperature. All this power and dominance makes it the color of royalty, courage, and wealth. It's also the color of succulence. Many fleshy and moist foods—tomatoes, strawberries, apples, and cherries—

Vibrant red-orange walls *have an energizing effect in this dining room. The scheme is conducive to animated discussions at meal times, and it even stimulates the appetite. This intense color palette pleases most people, but it should be used in areas of the home that are used for limited amounts of time.*

are red. However, it's a color with contradictions. For example, pink, a tint of red, symbolizes gentleness and femininity, while pure red is a color for military uniforms and stop signs. Vibrant and passionate, red is enjoyed by everyone, especially children, but its pure hue is seldom chosen for covering large surfaces because it is so powerful.

Yellow and Orange. Because these two colors also have long wavelengths, yellow and orange are just as stimulating as red, but they have their own unique qualities, too. Their excitement is festive and cheerful rather than bold and energetic, bright rather than purely stimulating. They are reminiscent of the warmth of sunshine and fire, late summer flowers, and precious metal. Both colors exist in many forms, from the faint yellow tint of peeled bananas to the deep golden hue of fall chrysanthemums, from the succulent red-orange of peaches to the flaming orange of autumn leaves. These colors enliven a space; this makes them excellent in rooms where food is served or where you want people to feel friendly and outgoing.

Various shades and tones of yellow create a cheerful ambiance in the room above.

A refreshing wash of lime green looks lush on the walls, right.

Green. Nature's dominant color, green symbolizes comfort and plenty. As such, it has many subtle and shifting but pleasing moods. It can be cool and restful and, at the same time, vital and lush. It ranges from the pale yellow-green of key limes through the bright yellow-green of Granny Smith apples to the rich green of emeralds and the deep green of forests and antique wine bottles. Green rooms tend toward a calm, relaxing ambiance. In fact, these qualities inspired the term "green room," which is used to signify a place in a theater where performers can unwind when off-stage.

Blue. Visible in both sky and water, blue can also be fresh, cool, and restful. However, its short wavelength makes it seem to recede; this creates the illusion of space and conjures images of shyness, reserve, formality, even haughtiness, and sometimes sadness. All this said, it's a favorite color because of those first associations, which make it easy on the eyes and nerves. Blues range from aquas and teals—the blue-greens that are more blue than green—through the blue-violets, all of which are excellent colors for use in rooms designed for relaxing or sleeping.

Calming blue walls can prove quiet and relaxing in a bedroom, above.

Shades of violet and red-violet look regal on an accent wall, below.

Violet. Violet, or purple, is often associated with passion. On the one hand it calls up images of lushness, regality, and emotion. On the other hand, its short wavelength—the shortest in the visible spectrum—make it recede visually. Maybe this complexity comes from the fact that violet links the warm and cool colors when you bend the visible spectrum into the color wheel. In its pure hue, violet is a difficult color to use in interior design except as an accent. However, its tints and shades, as well as the tints and shades of its analogous colors, red-violet and blue-violet, also make attractive and lively decorating colors.

Earth Tones. As a general description, earth tones comprise the browns and other neutrals found in nature. In terms of paint, they are tertiary and quaternary colors achieved by mixing various combinations of secondary, intermediate, and tertiary colors. They range from the pale cream of eggshells and the soft beige of

A combination of earth tones and shades of gray play up the look of textures in this contemporary bathroom. The muted quality of the color scheme appears understated and elegant.

sand through the rich browns of finished wood to the deep brown of tree bark and freshly turned earth. Their muted quality makes these hues gentle and understatedly elegant. However, they're often associated with texture. When they're combined with texture, including that achieved with decorative painting techniques, earth tones can become exciting and handsome. With or without texture, these colors make an effective background for bright hues.

Black and White. Black and white are complete opposites. Whereas white reflects all the colors of the visible spectrum, black absorbs them all. Thus they symbolize night and day, dark and light, bad and good, sad and happy. This intense, absolute contrast makes black and white dramatic together. Sophisticated and refined, they exemplify the epitome of style.

Developing Successful Color Schemes

Using colors that spontaneously attract you is a good idea because they make you feel comfortable naturally. So when you choose colors for your project, ask yourself questions. Do you really like these colors or are you drawn to them because they're new or trendy? Why do these colors move you? How do they make you feel? Can you live with them for a long time? In large amounts? Do they fit the style and purpose of your room?

Above all, don't make the beginner's sometimes expensive mistake of using a favorite color for everything without adding contrasts in texture, value, and intensity, and without providing accents. Otherwise, the color will lose its impact and become boring.

You can learn a great deal by studying color schemes around you. You can find wonderful inspiration in the creativity of other people as well as in nature. A study of

your surroundings demonstrates the infinite variety of successful color combinations available. Here are some places where you might begin to look:

Outdoors. You'll find color used at its best in nature, from the blossoms and foliage in gardens to birds overhead.

A vibrant flower garden, left, is a great place to look for color ideas.

Natural rock inspired a room's color scheme, below.

Museums and Art Books. All artwork is an excellent source of inspiration. Tapestries and paintings teach a lot, and the works of the French Impressionists are especially helpful. Fascinated by light, they discovered that colors placed side by side visually merge to create other colors when viewed from a distance. This experimentation resulted in paintings with great natural radiance, the kind of luminosity you want to achieve in your decorative painted finishes.

Fabrics. Patterned decorative fabrics, especially fine-quality ones, provide another good source of inspiration. Oriental rugs, upholstery, and curtain fabrics teach you about the control you can achieve by manipulating colors, values and intensities, and textures. Sample wallcovering books do some of the same; plus you may be able to borrow the books to take home for leisurely on-site study.

Decorating Magazines. Top designers create the rooms and product settings

featured in the articles and even the advertisements found in these publications. This makes them an excellent resource for viewing interiors executed by professionals with highly developed color skills. Likewise fashion magazines, because fashion design frequently anticipates where interior design will eventually wind up. Clip examples you like, and save them in a permanent color file.

Furniture Stores. Take time to stroll through the display rooms in stores that sell quality furniture. Created by trained designers, these spaces are intended to sell furniture, but they also show you about up-to-date uses of color.

Paint Color Systems. If you've ever wondered how many paint colors there are, just look at a paint manufacturer's color-chip system in a home center or paint store. The number of choices is incredible—one manufacturer offers over 6,000—but it also illustrates how many subtle variations can be achieved. These chips reinforce the lessons you've learned about color combinations and how they're affected by changes in value and intensity. Take home as many chips in as many colors as you can, and organize them into numerous color schemes. This is a good way to practice what you've learned.

Study all of these sources with a critical eye for two things: how to use value and intensity to modify hues, and how to play with proportions among various colors. Relate what you see to the color wheel, and memorize or otherwise note the combinations that you find particularly pleasing as well as appropriate for the setting in which you intend to use them.

Don't be afraid to copy. You'll find it's nearly impossible to reproduce a scheme exactly as you've seen it somewhere else because your room and furnishings aren't the same. As a result, you'll adapt and adjust much the same way you alter a new recipe when you try it. This natural adaptation lets your individuality emerge. In the process, be wary of popular color fads. Fads arise because manufacturers change colors every few years to sell their products. Colors may seem fresh or even slightly exotic when they first appear on the market, but they can soon become so prevalent that it's difficult to find merchandise in any other colors. Slowly, what once seemed new and exciting becomes common, tired, and old. To protect yourself from these constantly changing trends, choose only colors that you like and that work well in your home—whether or not they are currently in vogue. If you learn to use color adroitly, you'll never have to worry about getting bored with your scheme or being stuck with a room that appears dated.

Labels in image: BORDER, ACCENT COLORS, VALANCE, WALLPAPER, THROW PILLOWS, SOFA, ARMCHAIR, CARPET

Develop a color scheme with a sample board using fabric, trims, paint chips, wallpaper, and carpet pieces.

Developing Your Color Scheme

Start by considering how decorative painting techniques could enhance the room. But you can't decide what to paint or which technique and which colors to use without first considering many aspects about the room—its function, decorative style, size, architectural features, natural and artificial lighting, exposure to a view and weather, and traffic patterns. Is it a formal living room where you entertain sophisticated guests, or is it a comfortable family room where you want friends to feel welcome and relaxed? Maybe you'd like to make an infant's nursery light, soft, and pretty, or a child's playroom bold and energetic. Perhaps it's a warm south-facing sun room that could use a bit of visual cooling down, or a grand master bedroom that you'd like to make more personal and cozy.

Determine which of these influences are the most important; then select a technique and the colors that will reinforce your theme. The possibilities are limitless. Pull color ideas from drapery, upholstery fabric, or a painting; or use a neutral scheme overall, and accent it with a vibrant hue applied to woodwork or a piece of furniture.

Most effective design schemes combine no more than three colors and a neutral. Make this number work by using variations in value and intensity to create contrast among colors. Visualize where the hues fall on the color wheel and value scale. Then combine colors using the principles outlined here and the lessons you have learned. Some suggestions:

Monochromatic. Use one color in two or three different values—pale beige, light beige, and medium beige, for example—in two or three different proportions to create a two- or three-tone effect. The result is good texture contrast and color that glows.

Analogous. Use different values and proportions of three contiguous colors on the color wheel, or use different values and proportions of three neutrals. Using three pastels with the same value makes a harmonious combination that's easy on the eyes. The lighter the tint, the more compatible the colors. The same is true for the neutrals.

One Dominant Color. Use one color as the base of the technique and use its analogous, complementary, or split-complementary colors as accents within the scheme.

Two Dominant Colors. Use equal amounts of two colors drawn from common combinations, but harmonize them with contrasts in value and intensity. Or use them in equal strength over a neutral base coat, and blend them with a thin glaze or wash of the base coat.

Triad. Select three colors set equal distances apart on the color wheel. Let one color dominate. Use half as much of the second color, and use the third color as an accent.

13 Designer Techniques
For Manipulating Space with Color

Just as color has the power to produce physical and emotional changes, it also has the ability to visually mold space. It influences perceptions of size and shape, masks flaws, highlights good points, and creates harmony throughout a house.

1. *To alter a room's physical size, paint it a light, cool color to make it seem a bit larger and airier; a dark or warm color will make it seem smaller as well as cozier.*

2. *To warm north- or east-facing rooms, which tend to be cool and receive weak natural light, decorate them with light or bright and warm colors. To temper south-facing rooms, which tend to get hot (particularly in summer), or west-facing rooms, which are bright and warm (especially on summer afternoons), decorate with light, cool colors.*

3. *To raise a room's visual height, carry the wall color to the ceiling. Paint any crown or cove molding the same color as the walls.*

4. *To make a high ceiling appear lower or make a room feel more intimate, stop the wall's color 9 to 12 inches below the ceiling, and accent that line with a stenciled border, a wallpaper border, or molding. An alternative technique is to paint the ceiling with a subdued accent shade, bringing it onto the wall 9 to 12 inches below the ceiling line. Then accent the line with a border.*

5. *To coordinate a room completely, tint white ceiling paint slightly with a bit of the wall color.*

Splashes of color *applied in a random pattern warm up a large kitchen/family room, below.*

Thanks to color, a bench not only camouflages an ugly radiator but appears to blend into the walls, keeping a small hall from seeming crowded.

6. To camouflage an unsightly feature such as a radiator, paint it the same color as the walls so that it seems to disappear.

7. To highlight an attractive feature such as a paneled door, paint it a color that contrasts with the walls.

8. To provide control in a room decorated with bright, bold colors or many different colors, paint the woodwork, ceiling, and other architectural features white. This tones down the intense colors by giving the eye a place to rest.

9. To successfully paint your walls a dark or intense color, finish the project by sealing them with a non-yellowing clear top coat to magnify their depth and reflect light. This final step is especially important in small or dark rooms.

10. To unify a house with all-white or all-beige walls, use the same shade in all of the rooms.

11. To create harmony throughout a house, choose a signature color, and use it in some way in each room. Make it the dominant color in one room, the secondary color in another, the accent color in a third, an accessory color in a fourth, and so on.

12. To unify a house in which different hues have been used in each room, use neutral colors in transitional spaces such as hallways. This not only visually separates spaces but also prevents color clashes between rooms.

13. To keep decorative paint finishes from clashing where they meet, use the same technique to execute them, even if they contain different colors. Similar textures will help them blend.

COLOR'S VOCABULARY

Advancing colors: The warm colors. Like dark colors, they seem to advance toward you.

Analogous colors: Any three colors located next to one another on the color wheel.

Chroma: *See* Intensity.

Color scheme: A group of colors used together to create visual harmony in a space.

Color wheel: A circular arrangement of the 12 basic colors that shows how they relate to one another.

Complementary color: Colors located opposite one another on the color wheel.

Contrast: The art of assembling colors with different values and intensities in different proportions to create visual harmony in a color scheme.

Cool colors: The greens, blues, and violets.

Double-split complementary colors: The colors located on each side of two complementary colors on the color wheel.

Earth tones: The neutral colors that dominate in nature.

Hue: Synonym for color. Used most often to describe the color family to which a color belongs.

Intensity: The brightness or dullness of a color. Also referred to as a color's purity or saturation.

Intermediate colors: Red-orange, yellow-orange, yellow-green, blue-green, blue-violet, and red-violet; the six colors made by mixing equal amounts of a primary and secondary color.

Native colors: The basic inorganic pigments derived from minerals, used to make the colors found in artist's oil paints.

Pastel: A color to which a lot of white has been added to make it very light in value.

Primary colors: Red, yellow, and blue; the three colors in the visible spectrum that cannot be broken down into other colors. In various combinations and proportions, they make all other colors.

Quaternary colors: Colors made by mixing two tertiary colors.

Receding colors: The cool colors. Like light colors, receding colors make surfaces seem farther from the eye.

Secondary colors: Orange, green, and violet; the colors made by mixing equal amounts of two primary colors.

Shade: A color to which black has been added to make it darker.

Split complementary: A color paired with the colors on each side of its complementary color.

Tertiary colors: Colors made by combining two secondary colors.

Tint: A color to which white has been added to make it lighter in value.

Tone: A color to which gray has been added to change its value.

Triad: Any three colors located equidistant from one another on the color wheel.

Value: The lightness (tint or pastel) and darkness (shade) of a color.

Value scale: A graphic tool used to show the range of values between pure white and true black.

Visible spectrum: The bands of hues created when sunlight passes through a prism.

Warm colors: The reds, oranges, and yellows, as well as the browns.

CHAPTER 2

Color, paint, and glaze go hand in hand in decorative painting. Just as there is no color without hue, value, and intensity, there is no color in these techniques without paint and glaze. This elementary fact makes these media the most vital component in painting decorative finishes.

Fortunately, just as modern paint chemistry produces an unlimited array of beautiful colors at an affordable price, it also generates an astonishing collection of other easy-to-use coating and finishing products that take the tedium and excessive time out of the various decorative painting techniques. However, because you're going to be mixing and blending a lot of paint and glaze, it's essential that you understand precisely what these coatings are about.

Paints and Glazes, the Creative Media

An adept use of paints and glazes helped to create the exquisite look of aged plaster on this wall.

The Composition of Paint

Interior paint is a rather simple liquid product. It is an emulsion made of three ingredients: pigment, binder, and thinner.

Pigment is derived from natural or synthetic materials that have been ground into fine powders. Pigments give paint color. They can be combined to produce a specific hue and are then mixed with a binder. A *binder* is a viscous, pliant material that holds pigments in suspension and makes them adhere to surfaces. Rather than dissolving, the pigments stay suspended in this binder, which is the reason you always have to stir paint (to remix the pigments with the binder) before applying it. A *thinner* is a substance used to dilute the mixture of pigments and binder in order to make it spreadable.

Paint Types

The paint industry uses two kinds of binders in interior paints: *latex* and *alkyd*. Their names are often used to describe the paint.

Latex. These paints contain either acrylic or vinyl resins or a combination of the two. The type of resin determines the paint's quality. High-quality latex paints contain 100 percent acrylic resin. They are the most expensive, but their highly durable finish also makes them the best type of latex paint to use for decorative finishes. Medium-cost latex paints contain a blend of acrylic and vinyl resins; they're acceptable for decorative finishes. Moderate-cost latex paints contain 100 percent vinyl resin, which does not produce the required durable surface. Don't use them for decorative finishes. To thin any latex paint, use water.

Alkyd. These paints contain a number of artificial resins called alkyds, which have replaced the linseed oil formerly used as a binder in oil-based interior paint. Sometimes these alkyds are combined with vegetable oil to improve their performance. People tend to use the terms "alkyd" and "oil-based" interchangeably. Today, calling an interior paint oil-based is just another way of saying it's an alkyd paint, although technically that's incorrect. The term "oil-based" is used throughout this book to avoid confusion because many of the products used in conjunction with alkyd paint do have an oil base and may be solvent-soluble.

Use petroleum solvents to thin alkyd paints. All of alkyd paint's adjunct products also are solvent-soluble.

Other Types. In addition to pigments, binder, and thinner, each type of paint may contain special additives designed to tailor them to paint a specific surface. *Rust inhibitors*, for example, go into paints for metal surfaces that may corrode; *texturing compounds* go into paints where a rough, grained, or dimensional quality is desired.

Comparisons. Each paint type has advantages and disadvantages. Because of its water base, latex paint dries quickly and cleans up easily with soap and water. It also has little or no odor and is nonflammable and safe to use. The

A watercolor effect, created by artist Lucianna Samu, distinguishes this wall mural.

quick drying time reduces the waiting between coats; unfortunately, it also leaves less time for working a complicated technique such as marbling. And though latex paint cleans up easily when wet, it becomes quite permanent when dry. Water won't be enough to clean it up: You'll have to use denatured alcohol (or a utility knife) to remove dried splatters and spills. Latex paint also produces a more opaque finish than that of alkyd paint.

Like the old oil-based paints it replaced, alkyd paint dries more slowly. This gives you more time to work on a finish, but it also means the paint has time to sag on a vertical surface if not correctly applied. Drying time can be as long as 24 hours between coats, longer in humid weather. In addition, alkyd paint has a strong odor, must be thinned and cleaned up with mineral spirits or another petroleum-based solvent, and is highly flammable, which requires you to take safety precautions. (See "Personal Safety" in Chapter 3, page 77.) The petroleum solvents used to make alkyd paint spreadable cause these disadvantages.

Four types of paint finishes in descending order—eggshell, flat, semigloss, and gloss. They range from matted to shiny.

Petroleum solvents cause another problem, too. They contain volatile organic compounds (VOCs) that evaporate into the atmosphere as they dry. Once in the air, they help produce lower-atmospheric ozone, a major agent in creating smog. To protect the atmosphere, air pollution laws in California and many other communities across the country now restrict the extensive use of alkyd paint. In response to these restrictions, the paint industry has reduced the amount of solvent in alkyd paint from an average 50 percent to an average 20 percent in recent years, and it is looking for ways to reduce it further. But eliminating solvents outright hasn't yet proved possible. Despite their environmental disadvantage, they do give alkyd paint several desirable qualities, such as improving its ability to accept color pigments and helping it to produce a permanent film and better leveling. Check with your local building inspection department, community public health department, or state pollution-control agency to learn about your region's regulations. If it does place restrictions, water-soluble painting and coating products make effective substitutes.

Paint Finishes

Each type of paint, regardless of its formula, produces a film, or finish, and a sheen when dry. The sheens range from matte to shiny and are described by generic names. *Flat paint* has a nonreflective, matte sheen; *eggshell* and *satin paints* have a finish with a sheen that is soft, lustrous, and light-reflecting, although the satin finish is a little more lustrous and reflective and a little less porous than the eggshell; *semigloss paint* has a slightly glossy sheen that is light reflective; and *gloss paint* produces a hard, shiny sheen that reflects the maximum amount of light. All the non-matte paints contain gloss additives so they dry to a hard finish and are classed as enamels. As a paint's gloss level increases, so does its durability and scrubbability, but it also becomes harder, slicker, and less absorbent.

Each type of finish affects decorative paint techniques in specific ways. A *flat-finish base coat*, for example, is porous, so it absorbs glaze. This absorbency means a glaze dries faster, which limits your working time and makes removing wet glazes almost impossible. However, it also has the advantage of blending a glaze into the base coat, making the two elements seem like one. This keeps the base coat from showing through as a separate color and softens or diffuses any pattern by diluting it somewhat. An *eggshell* or *satin base coat* is nonporous, so it allows a glaze to stay wet longer, giving you more working time and making removal possible. Because the glaze stays on top of the base coat, however, its pattern appears sharply defined, and the pure base-coat color shows through, producing a nice contrast.

Which finish is best for a base coat? That depends on your project and the effect you're trying to create. However, a flat or eggshell finish works well for the base coat of most projects. Professional decorative painters sometimes consider a satin finish too slippery. The same may be said of semigloss and gloss finishes, although they make excellent base coats for faux stone techniques.

A glazed wall with a semigloss finish displays a rich textural look.

Glazed walls and faux granite cabinets enhance a large open-plan kitchen and family room.

Both latex and alkyd paints adhere and cover well and produce a durable finish. Use either type for base coats. However, every other paint product—additional paints, colorants, thinners, glazes, and top coats—that you apply on top of an alkyd base coat must be oil-based and solvent-soluble. Why? Because water-based latex and acrylic paints will have very poor adhesion to an oil-based surface. The reverse is not true, however. You can top coat a latex base coat with oil-based, solvent-soluble products if the latex coat is completely dry. Note that "completely dry" is the operative phrase here. Once dry, a latex paint contains no water to react with the oil. A latex base coat will also need a latex primer; an alkyd base coat could go over a latex or alkyd primer.

See Chapter Four, "Surface Preparation: Building Your Base," pages 101–103, for instructions on how to apply a base coat properly and how to hold a brush and a roller to produce a consistent, even stroke.

Undercoats

Unless you're applying a base coat to a previously painted surface, you should use a sealer or a primer to prepare the surface for painting. Basically, sealers and primers have the same function. They prepare a surface for painting by providing a slightly coarse surface that gives the paint something on which to grab. Called *tooth*, this coarse quality improves the performance, appearance, and longevity of paint. However, sealers and primers accomplish the job in slightly different ways, and that creates some confusion about which one to use. The best way to decide is to remember this slogan: Sealers seal, primers prepare.

A diverse mixture of techniques—antiquing, glazing, and stenciling—add old-fashioned charm to the walls and objects in this room.

Sealers

Sealers do just what their name implies. They seal porous surfaces by forming a durable, nonabsorbent barrier that prevents their sucking up paint. Use a sealer if the surface to be painted is one of the following:

- Bare or raw open-grained woods such as oak and maple, because their porous cell structure absorbs paint and glaze
- Highly colored bare or raw woods such as redwood, because their resins bleed through and stain paint
- Bare or raw wood with knots, because the oily resin in the knots rejects paint
- A surface with oily stains such as crayon, because they bleed through paint with time
- A surface covered with spots of mold or mildew
- Large patches of porous joint compound or patching plaster
- Highly porous masonry products such as unglazed brick, cinder block, or concrete
- Metal surfaces requiring the use of corrosion inhibitors

Failure to seal such surfaces against absorbency before painting results in a rough, uneven, dull paint finish that cannot be eliminated with additional coats of paint.

A faux birchwood finish allows this fireplace to stand out. Prime all surfaces before painting stripped woodwork.

Sealers come in latex and alkyd formulations. Acrylic latex sealers perform as well as alkyd sealers. It's a good idea to use a sealer containing the same binder as your base coat paint. If your base coat is a deep, dark, or very bright color, have the sealer tinted at 50 to 75 percent of the base color.

Shellac. This is another superior sealer. It's frequently used to seal porous surfaces, such as joint compound, patching plaster, and open-grained wood, and difficult spots such as oily stains and mildew. It dries quickly and is not suitable for use overlarge areas. Shellac is made from the secretion of a tropical bug dissolved in alcohol. It comes in three colors: *clear*, which dries transparent and is sometimes labeled "white"; *opaque* or *chalked white*, often referred to as white-pigmented shellac; and *orange* or *blond*. The most useful form for sealing is a commercial 4-pound cut, white-pigmented shellac sold as a combination sealer/primer for tough-to-cover surfaces—it should be thinned with denatured alcohol. Once it's dry, you can paint over shellac with latex or alkyd paint.

Primers

Primers prepare surfaces for painting by making them more uniform in texture and giving them tooth. They dry more quickly and cost less than paint. In fact, by tinting your primer you can save on additional base coats. Primers also adhere to a previously painted, dirty, or repaired surface.

Prime all unpainted surfaces before base coating, except those itemized under "Sealers," on page 45. This includes existing woodwork stripped of its original finish. It's always best to prime over existing finishes, especially when one of the following conditions exists:

- Large sections have been repaired with porous joint compound or patching plaster, in which case you'll have to apply a sealer and then prime
- The existing paint has worn thin and you want a like-new painted surface
- The existing paint doesn't pass an absorption test. Try this: Apply a patch of mineral spirits to a small section; if it doesn't stay wet for at least 2 or 3 minutes, you should prime the surface
- The existing surface is a very bright, deep, or dark color and you plan to cover it with a much lighter shade of paint
- Your base coat is a very bright, deep, or dark color, in which case you should have your primer tinted at 50 to 75 percent of the base-coat color

Like sealers, primers come in latex and alkyd formulations. Remember, a primer is chosen for its compatibility with what already exists on the surface and what you intend to apply. If the existing finish is an alkyd paint, apply a latex primer before painting over with a latex product, and vice versa.

An acid-green glaze looks almost hot in a remodeled kitchen. The flat finish plays off the glossy white tiles nicely.

A thinner glaze formula results in a cool, almost watery appearance on these walls. The "drapery" is actually trompe l'oeil.

Acrylic craft paints

Colorants

Today's interior paints come in such a wide variety of colors that, theoretically at least, it's possible to create your color scheme using nothing but these custom-mixed paints. By selecting carefully from a paint manufacturer's color-chip system you can get what you want in the exact values and intensities desired without having to mix paints yourself. Certainly that's a time-saver as well as a safety net for selecting the right color. However, much of the fun of the various decorative painting techniques lies in developing your own paints and glazes. You can do this by using a colorant suited to the type of paint or glazing medium you're applying. The following colorants are commonly employed in mixing paints for decorative finishes.

Artist's Acrylic Paints. These paints contain pigments suspended in acrylic resin, a formula similar to that of latex paint, only of much higher quality. Obviously, the acrylic content makes them ideal for coloring latex paints and water-soluble glazes. The basic color palette includes lampblack (or bone or ivory black), titanium white, raw umber, burnt umber, raw sienna, burnt sienna, yellow ochre, yellow oxide, chrome yellow medium, red ochre, red oxide, chrome orange, cadmium orange, alizarin crimson, vermillion red, cadmium red, ultramarine blue, and chrome green medium. Artist's acrylics dry quickly and can be layered on top of one another. Sold at craft shops and art-supply stores, these colorants come in tubes and jars. The tubes give you good control, letting you squeeze out paint drop by drop. Eight-ounce tubes are the most economical.

Universal Tints. Usable in both water-based and oil-based paints and in glaze mediums, universal tints are pigments combined with ethylene glycol and a little water. These are the colorants paint retailers use to custom-mix paint colors. They're ideal for large projects or ones involving an extreme color change because they are less expensive than artist's acrylics. They come in economical 16-ounce bottles. If you need a smaller amount, such as just a few ounces, your paint store can fill a small bottle that has a nozzle cap with the amount you need. The nozzle cap lets you add the tint drop by drop.

Another important point: After each use, cover and store these tints well—preferably upside down.

Universal tints have two drawbacks compared with acrylics. First, they offer less of a color range, although they do include the same basic color palette as artist's acrylics. Second, they don't contain a dryer. Don't let them constitute more than 10 to 20 percent of your paint unless you also add a dryer to the mixture.

Artist's Oil Paints. These are typically the tube paints you associate with fine-art paintings, but they can come in the form of pigment sticks, as well. Consisting of pigments suspended in linseed oil, artist's oil paints come in a wide range of saturated colors, including the same basic color palette as artist's acrylics and universal tints. They dry to a lustrous sheen. Despite the fact that they're expensive and slow-drying, they work well for tinting alkyd paints and solvent-soluble glazes.

Japan Colors. Japan colors are your best choice for tinting alkyd paints and solvent-soluble glazes, but these concentrated lacquer-based colorants are hard to find in many areas: Try art-supply stores serving the sign-painting trade and mail-order art-supply companies. Japan colors come in cans, which give you less control than tubes; they have intense, flat color and dry quickly.

Pigment stick oil paints

Artist's oils in a tube

**Dry-ground pigments
and egg tempera**

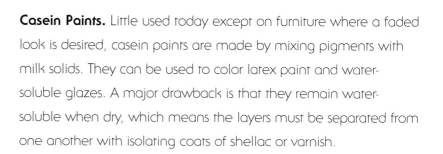

Casein Paints. Little used today except on furniture where a faded look is desired, casein paints are made by mixing pigments with milk solids. They can be used to color latex paint and water-soluble glazes. A major drawback is that they remain water-soluble when dry, which means the layers must be separated from one another with isolating coats of shellac or varnish.

Tempera Paints. The paints of schoolchildren, tempera paints are a mixture of pigments and an egg-oil emulsion. They, too, remain water-soluble when dry, so layers must be separated from one another by a layer of shellac or varnish. That's one reason this type isn't used for coloring latex paints or water-soluble glazes.

Washes and Glazes

Many of the decorative painting techniques acquire their unique character with washes and glazes. A *wash* is a thinned-out latex or acrylic paint; a *glaze* is a paint or colorant mixed with a transparent glazing medium and diluted with a thinner that has the same solubility as the colorant and the medium. Each type has its own look and is suitable for specific decorative finishes. A wash produces a flat, gauzy film of color that is akin to placing a layer of organdy over a fabric. You make it by simply thinning colored latex paint, artist's acrylic, or universal tint with water. This produces a sheer film of paint that lets some of the base-coat color show through. How much shows through depends on how much the paint is diluted.

An extremely thin wash is messy to apply—you'll get a quick-drying medium suitable for simple techniques such as sponging and color washing. If you want to slow down the drying time, add a retardant—many types are available where you buy your paint supplies. The finish will be beautiful but not durable.

More complex than a wash, a glaze produces a translucent, luminous finish. A good glaze should:

- Contain easily available, inexpensive materials that produce a consistent product
- Produce a smooth medium that clings to surfaces, especially vertical surfaces, without sagging or slumping
- Offer adequate working time
- Dry overnight

The translucent glazing medium, which is nothing more than paint without pigment, is responsible for the final finish. Translucent glaze media come in both latex and alkyd formulations, so you have plenty from which to choose to create your desired effect. To make a glaze, simply mix paint or another type of colorant with a translucent glazing medium, and then thin the mixture to the desired consistency with water or mineral spirits as appropriate. (See "Thinners," on page 53, for more guidance.)

Transparent Acrylic Gel. This glazing medium makes a water-soluble glaze. You can find it in art supply stores, craft shops, and stores servicing the painting trade. You add color to transparent acrylic gel by mixing it with any water-soluble colorant such as latex paint, artist's acrylics, universal tints, tempera paints, or casein paints. (Note, however, that the last two products dry flat and opaque and result in finishes that are less permanent than glazes tinted with artist's acrylics or universal tints.) To thin the mixture, use water. The amount of water will determine the degree of sheen on the finished result. This medium dries quickly, but you can add a retardant to help extend its drying time if you feel that it's necessary. Transparent acrylic gel is a suitable glazing medium for all the decorative painting techniques.

The glazing
medium is colorless, but you
can add colorant. Make the
mixture as thin and translucent
as you like.

After mixing the glazing medium with the colorant in a bucket, pour it into a paint tray.

Latex Glazing Liquid. Sometimes labeled acrylic glaze, this glazing medium is similar to acrylic gel medium. It is a water-based glaze suitable for basic finishes such as sponging, ragging, and simple marbling techniques. You can color it and thin it the same way you do acrylic gel. It is a suitable glazing medium for all of the decorative painting techniques.

Commercial Oil Glaze. This is a ready-mixed product sold in cans at paint and art-supply stores. It comes in basic colors and several sheens. Use it straight from the can, or thin it with mineral spirits as desired. Just be sure the solvent doesn't constitute more than 10 percent of the glaze formula, or the mixture will get too runny. In addition to its translucence, a commercial oil glaze has the advantage of remaining wet longer, giving you more working time. This glazing medium is suitable for all of the decorative painting techniques.

Alkyd Glazing Liquid. This is the most widely used oil-based glazing medium because it is so easy to mix, so workable, and so reliable. A standard oil-glaze formula uses equal parts solvent-soluble colorant (colored alkyd paints, universal tints, artist's oil paints, or japan colors), alkyd glazing liquid, and mineral spirits. This mixture dries slowly, so you have adequate working time for longer techniques. If you want it to dry faster and to produce a harder finish, add more mineral spirits instead of more alkyd glazing liquid. It is suitable for all the decorative painting techniques.

See Chapter Five, "Mixing Paints and Glazes," starting on page 107, for instructions on mixing paints and glazes. Use the glaze formula and application method for each technique in "Part II: The Decorative Painting Techniques," beginning on page 125.

Thinners

A number of volatile solvents are used to thin and clean the alkyd paints and glazing media used in decorative painting. Of all of them, white mineral spirits works the best. It evaporates quickly and uniformly, doesn't disturb dry layers of paint under it, doesn't leave a gummy residue as it evaporates or react chemically with other ingredients, and is relatively inexpensive. However, it does have several disadvantages. The least of these is its petroleum distillate odor. (Fortunately, it's far less offensive than that of most other solvents.) Also, its vapors can ignite if they come into contact with an open flame, and it's slightly toxic if swallowed. Both problems are not difficult to avoid by using common sense. Buy it as generic 100-percent white mineral spirits or as paint thinner, which is basically the same product.

Boiled linseed oil and turpentine are effective substitutes for mineral spirits, but they are far more expensive. A small amount of boiled linseed oil improves the flow and gloss of alkyd paints, and it's frequently used in the glazes employed in the wood-graining techniques. Never throw rags soaked with linseed oil in the trash—they can self-combust. Dry them outside before discarding.

Thinning an acrylic glaze with water resulted in the three different levels of translucency used on these boxes.

Clear Top Coats

A clear top coat is just that—a transparent finishing layer of protection applied on top of many decorative painted finishes. It gives your decorated surface any degree of sheen you want as well as protecting it from fading, wear, and tear. Many decorative painting techniques—sponging, color washing, and stenciling are three examples—produce a durable surface by themselves and don't require a clear top coat. As a general rule, applying a top coat to such finishes is optional, based on whether or not you want them to shine. However, you might apply a clear top coat as protection over any decorative painted surface in hard-use living areas, such as an informal eating area or a child's bedroom, especially on tabletops, countertops, woodwork, doors, and floors, which are prone to nicks, scratches, and other damage.

However, complex finishes such as faux marble and wood grain always require a clear top coat. It gives them a depth that adds to their realism as well as providing protection and sheen. Instructions for each finish presented in "Part II: The Decorative Painting Techniques," beginning on page 125, includes recommendations regarding the need for a clear top coat.

Hard-use surfaces, *such as this floor painted by artist Lucianna Samu, should always receive a protective top coat.*

There are many kinds of clear top coats on the market. They come with both oil/alkyd and water bases, and some have a full range of surface finishes—matte, eggshell, satin, semigloss, and gloss. Choose a top-coat product based on the degree of shine you want on your completed project. For example, if your wall has imperfections, you probably will go to great lengths to hide them by using a flat paint and a flat glaze. Sealing that finish with a gloss top coat will defeat your efforts because the shine will highlight every flaw in the surface. Sealing and applying a clear top coat or polyurethane finish should be limited to surfaces other than walls.

Oil varnish, polyurethane, acrylic varnish, refined white beeswax, and *shellac* are the most common clear top-coat products used in interior decorative painting. The inevitable yellowing of many of these products is the bane of all the decorative painting techniques. This discoloration varies widely, even between brands within a product group, with the alkyd-based top coats yellowing more readily than the water-based products. Those that yellow heavily make poor choices for sealing work in white, pastels, or subtle color combinations unless, by chance, the colors are compatible with yellow. Fortunately, they do not affect black and dark colors to the same degree. Ask your paint dealer for suggestions. Also, read the labels to learn about yellowing, drying times, and coverage recommendations for individual brands and products.

Oil Varnish. This is the traditional top coat used in decorative painting. Its big disadvantage is the fact that it yellows with age, especially in rooms that receive little sunlight. This yellowing distorts the color under the varnish. (Think of what would happen to your color if you added a few drops of yellow to it during mixing.) Also, varnish usually overpowers finishes executed in delicate and subtle colorations.

Oil varnish is compatible with alkyd paints and oil-based glazes. You can also use it over latex paint and a water-based glaze once they are completely dry. Thin this varnish with mineral spirits

A clear top coat enhances the wood-grain effect incorporated into this gameboard, which has been painted on a boy's bedroom floor.

PRODUCT COMPATIBILITY AT A GLANCE

Use this quick reference guide to select products with the same solubility. Products with the same solubility successfully combine with one another whether you're mixing them together or layering them on top of one another. Usually, you'll have to separate those with different solubilities from one another by applying an isolating layer of shellac or varnish. The one exception is when you use solvent-soluble products, which you can apply over water-soluble products once they're completely dry. Shellac is not listed here because it is alcohol-soluble and may be used as an isolating layer between both water-soluble and solvent-soluble products.

WATER-SOLUBLE	SOLVENT-SOLUBLE
Undercoats	
Polyvinyl acetate (PVA) sealers	Alkyd sealers
Latex primers	Alkyd primers
Paints	
Latex interior paints	Alkyd interior paints
Colorants	
Artist's acrylics	Artist's oil paints
Universal tints	Universal tints
Casein	Japan colors
Tempera	
Glaze Mediums	
Transparent acrylic gel	Commercial oil glaze
Latex glazing liquid	Alkyd glazing liquid
Thinners	
Water	Mineral spirits
	Paint thinner
	Turpentine
	Boiled linseed oil
Top Coats	
Acrylic varnish	Oil varnish
Water-based polyurethane	Polyurethane

or paint thinner. It dries to the touch in about 3 hours and dries completely in 12 to 24 hours, depending on heat and humidity. The greater the oil content, the brighter the gloss and the slower the drying time. All oil varnishes yellow with time, but marine varnish is the worst offender and is not recommended for use over decorative finishes.

Polyurethane. This product makes a good top coat for most types of paint except artist's oils. Thin it with mineral spirits. Each coat requires 12 hours of drying time. While it yellows less than oil varnish, it still isn't a good choice for use over white, pastels, and subtle color combinations.

Acrylic Varnish. Based on the same medium used to make water-soluble glazes, this finish works only over water-based products. Do not apply it over alkyd paint, even if the paint is completely dry. Obviously, you can thin it with water. Apply it using a roller; a brush can leave marks. Acrylic varnish dries quickly and yellows only slightly.

Water-Based Polyurethane. This product is much like acrylic varnish, only stronger, and it takes a few minutes longer to dry. Because it works only on water-based paints and glazes, thin it with water, and apply it using a roller. It produces no yellowing.

Shellac. Shellac doesn't make a good top coat because it produces a soft finish that's easily damaged by abrasion, heat, water, and alcohol. However, it does makes an excellent isolating layer between layers of glaze. It's also a superior sealer and primer for small areas and furniture. Shellac yellows as much as oil-based top coats.

Refined White Beeswax. An expensive product, refined white beeswax produces an elegant, lustrous finish that doesn't yellow. However, it's more labor-intensive to apply than other clear finishes. You have to rub it on with a clean, lint-free cloth, let it set, and then hand-buff it to a translucent glow with another clean cloth. You'll also have to reapply it regularly. This labor-intensiveness is why it's mostly used as a top coat for wood furniture. When you're ready to apply a fresh coat, you can easily remove the old wax using mineral spirits or wood cleaner without disturbing the paint finish under it.

Understand that with most clear finishes, the more coats you apply, the more yellowing that occurs. Balance this disadvantage against the final appearance you're aiming for and the degree of protection your finish needs. Make this decision in the beginning when you're planning what you'd like to do, not after you've finished.

Clear paste wax, applied with a soft cloth, can be used to clean and polish wood surfaces or objects, such as this painted candlestick. It will yellow slightly over time. White beeswax, which comes in blocks that must be melted down to liquid form, remains clear.

How Much and How Long

Check the labels on paint, glazing medium, and top-coat containers to determine their recommended coverage. For example, most paints can cover 350 to 400 square feet per gallon, but it's safer to plan on coverage of 300 square feet per gallon and 75 square feet per quart. Always buy and mix more paint and glaze than you need. A general rule of thumb is to add 10 percent to your estimate and round up to the next highest quart.

You need this extra paint or glaze for several reasons. First, you don't want to risk running out in mid-wall. Even a subtle difference in color between two batches can make it necessary to repaint the entire surface. Even if your luck holds and the two different batches match exactly (which is rare), you have still failed to keep a wet edge on your paint or glaze. (See Chapter Four, "Surface Preparation: Building Your Base," starting on page 78.) Because the paint or glaze will begin to dry while you're mixing the new batch, you'll get an unattractive dark line where you butt the second batch against the first.

Second, you should allow extra for spills, waste, and porous spots (even entire surfaces) that absorb more: Plaster is far more absorbent than wallboard, for example, so it always requires more paint. Besides, you probably want some paint left over for touching up. You may even want to use the same color in an adjoining room in the future.

Two-toned glazed stripes cover the portion of the wall above the chair rail only, so the artist divided the square footage of the room in half when estimating how much paint would be needed for the job.

Follow these steps to determine how much paint, glaze, or top coat is needed:

1. Measure the length of all the walls of the room or surface to calculate its perimeter. Add these figures together. For example, if you're painting the walls in a room that measures 12 feet wide and 15 feet long, calculate its perimeter this way: 12 + 12 + 15 + 15 = 54 feet.

2. Multiply the perimeter by the wall height to get the area in square feet. If the room is 8 feet high, calculate its area this way: 54 x 8 = 432 square feet.

3. Subtract 21 square feet for each standard-size door and 15 square feet for each window, and the actual area of architectural features such as fireplaces, bookcases, cabinets, or archways that won't be painted. If you're painting a room that has two windows and two doors, that's 15 + 15 + 21 + 21 = 72. Then adjust the square footage this way: 432 –72 = 360 square feet.

Subtract doorways, windows, and cabinets from your estimate.

4. Multiply the adjusted square footage by 10 percent to allow for the necessary overage: 360 x 0.10 = 36 square feet. Add this to the adjusted square footage to get the final square footage: 360 + 36 = 396.

5. Divide the final square footage by 300, the amount of space adequately covered by one gallon of paint, to get the number of gallons needed: 396/300 = 1 gallon and 1-plus quarts (75 square feet plus 21 square feet left over). Round up to the next quart, and buy 1 gallon plus 2 quarts. (Round up to the next full gallon if the calculations show you need 3 quarts.)

Storing and Disposing of Paint

Store newly purchased paint in a warm, dry, preferably dim or dark place situated well away from open flame. Above all, never store paint on porches, in garages, attics, or storage sheds, or in other unheated places where it might freeze. In addition, keep it out of the reach of children and pets.

If you have paint left over after your project, store it the same way: in a can, preferably the one in which it came. Clean the excess paint from the can's rim with a wet paper towel, put the lid in place, and tightly seal it by tapping around the rim with a rubber mallet or a hammer and board.

An interior-grade latex paint with a semigloss finish takes less than half a day to dry completely.

If you want to dispose of leftover paint, keep in mind that most liquid paint products, including latex paint, mineral spirits, and paint thinners, are considered household hazardous wastes. That makes them subject to your community's rules governing their correct disposal. Do not put them into the trash or pour them down the drain, into a storm sewer, or onto the ground. Instead, you have the following disposal options:

- Seal the paint can as described above, and take it to the nearest authorized hazardous waste disposal site.
- Seal the can as described above, and give it to a civic or charitable organization that can use it.
- If it's a small amount of leftover paint, brush it on scrap cardboard, let it dry, and toss the cardboard into the trash.
- Check the paint label. You may be able to fill the can with cat litter or shredded newspaper, let it set up, and then throw it into the trash.
- Pour dirty mineral spirits and other solvents into a can containing a little water, seal the lid tightly, and take it to a hazardous waste disposal site.
- Wipe out the insides of empty cans and buckets with newspaper or paper towels.

- Let paint-soiled newspapers, paper towels, rags, plastic sheeting, and other debris dry completely before putting it in the trash.
- Hang solvent-soaked rags outdoors to dry before disposing of them, or place them in gallon cans half-filled with water, seal them well, and place them in the trash. Never bunch wet solvent-soaked rags together in a bag or box and set aside until trash removal day. Petroleum solvents produce heat as they dry (evaporate), and the rags can easily spontaneously combust.

Drying Times

Don't rush a decorative paint finish. Your project's success depends on allowing its surface to dry thoroughly before going on to the next step. So always allow sufficient drying time for each coat. Even latex paints need time to dry.

Actually, you will deal with two types of "dry": *dry to the touch* and *cured*, or thoroughly dry, also often referred to as the *recoating time*. Cured means the paint is permanent; it will not absorb more moisture. Because paint dries from the outer surface in, it can feel dry on the top (dry to the touch) while it's still wet underneath. Each layer must be thoroughly cured before applying another layer. Follow the recommended drying times specified on the paint's label, or use the chart on this page as a guide to estimate average drying times when you're planning your project's time frame.

Coating a surface that's dry to the touch but uncured causes the top layer to bubble, crack, or peel. Distressing a

AVERAGE DRYING TIMES

Normal drying conditions assume a 77-degree Fahrenheit temperature and 50-percent relative humidity. A higher or lower temperature and humidity level affects drying time significantly. Do not apply interior paint when the temperature is less than 50 degrees Fahrenheit.

BASE COAT	DRY TO THE TOUCH	CURED
Interior Paints		
Latex, flat	20 minutes to 1 hour	1 to 3 hours
Latex, eggshell	2 hours	4 to 6 hours
Latex, satin	2 hours	4 to 6 hours
Alkyd, eggshell	5 hours	24 hours or more
Alkyd, satin	5 hours	24 hours or more
Interior Enamels		
Latex, semigloss	45 minutes	4 to 8 hours
Latex, gloss	2 hours	24 hours or more
Alkyd, semigloss	4 hours	24 hours or more
Alkyd, gloss	4 hours	24 hours or more

glaze applied over an uncured base coat breaks that base coat's skin, which allows the wet paint to bleed into the glaze and ruin your finish.

Many factors influence drying time. For example, it's greatly affected by the use of colorants and may never dry if too much is used. The amount of light, the type of weather, the atmospheric humidity, air movement—they all count. For example, paint doesn't dry as quickly in a dark or humid room as it does in a sunny, airy room with low humidity. A paint's surface sheen also alters drying time. (See the box "Average Drying Times," on page 61.) Flat paint dries more quickly than satin or semigloss paint. Other influences include the surface's absorbency, the paint's thickness, the type of thinner used, and the colorant used.

There are times when you want to slow down or speed up drying time. Slowing down the process gives you more time to work on a technique; speeding it up allows you to apply the next coat sooner.

To speed up the drying time for both types of paint, you might use an oscillating fan in the room, but that could raise dust that can settle on your wet surface. A hand-held electric hair dryer will speed up the drying process for small projects and samples.

To slow down the drying time of alkyd paint, add boiled linseed oil or turpentine to it. Be careful to add it sparingly, though. The more you use, the glossier the finish gets. You can also add products called dryers or siccatives, which are metallic salts (such as cobalt stannate) that speed drying by introducing more oxygen into the paint film. Burnt umber and raw umber contain manganese salts that act as dryers.

To slow the drying time for water-soluble glazes, dampen the wall with a moist sponge before you start painting, or use a humidifier to raise the room's humidity before starting the project. You might also try blocking direct sunlight from entering the room. Adding a little acrylic gel retardant to the glaze also works, but this weakens a paint or glaze if the retardant exceeds 10 percent of the formula. Adding a small amount of water is the least expensive way to keep the glaze wet. Just be sure you don't make it too runny.

Handling Spills and Spatters

Every project is easier if you wipe up drips and splatters as you go along. But different types of paint have specific clean-up requirements as well.

Water-based Products. If you're using water-based paints, keep a bucket of water and some clean rags nearby so that you can quickly wipe up mistakes as they happen. If paint gets on carpeting or other fabric, pick it up by dabbing it with a slightly damp sponge. Don't rub it. Rubbing works the paint into the fabric's weave, and it will never come out. If you miss a spot and it dries over several days, wipe it off with denatured alcohol. Rub lightly so you don't damage the paint underneath. If the paint dries on fabric, try removing it with a commercial spot remover or water-wash brush cleaner.

Oil-based Products. If you're using alkyd paints, keep some mineral spirits and clean rags nearby to wipe up spots as soon as they occur on hard surfaces. If the paint splatters on carpeting or fabric, dab it up with a clean rag slightly dampened with paint thinner. Do not rub the spot. Rubbing works the paint into the fabric's weave. If the paint dries on the fabric, try removing it with a commercial alkyd brush cleaner. Test the cleaner in an inconspicuous spot first to determine the fabric's colorfastness and tolerance.

Painting wood trim can be tedious. If the paint spatters onto adjacent surfaces, clean it up immediately.

PAINT'S VOCABULARY

Acrylic: A high-quality synthetic resin used as a binder in latex paint.

Additive: Ingredients added to a basic paint formula so it performs specific tasks such as adding texture to a wall or inhibiting corrosion.

Adhesion: The ability of paint to stick to a surface when dry.

Alkyd: A solvent-soluble medium that uses artificial resins (called *alkyds*) as a binder. Also called "oil-based." It is thinned with petroleum solvents, linseed oil, or turpentine.

Artist's acrylic: Pigment suspended in acrylic resin. Comes in tubes. Used as a latex colorant.

Artist's oil paint: Traditional oil-based artist's paint. Comes in tubes. Used as a alkyd colorant.

Binder: Viscous, pliant liquid that holds paint's pigments in suspension.

Bite: The ability of a paint to adhere to a surface.

Casein paint: A faded-looking, water-soluble paint made with pigments and milk solids.

Colorants: Various forms of pigments used to add color to paints and glazes.

Cured: Paint that is thoroughly dry and ready to be recoated.

Custom-mixed: Paint with color that's been mixed in a paint store to the exact color specified in a paint manufacturer's color-chip system.

Eggshell: A nonporous paint finish that has a low luster or soft sheen.

Enamel: Paint that has finely ground pigments and a high binder content so it dries to a hard, scrubbable, semigloss or gloss finish.

Finish: The sheen and porosity produced by a paint's surface when dry.

Flammable: Something that's capable of easily catching on fire.

Flat: A matte paint finish that doesn't reflect light.

Glaze: A translucent medium for decorative finishes.

Glazing medium: A translucent binder used to make glazes. It is paint without pigment.

Gloss: A finish that's shiny and reflects light.

Hide: The ability of a paint to cover a surface so what's underneath doesn't show through.

Japan color: Oil-based pigments. Comes in strong colors. Used as a colorant.

Latex: A water-soluble paint made with an acrylic or vinyl resin binder. It is thinned with water.

Leveling: The ability of a paint to level out to a smooth surface so there are no brush or roller marks when it is dry.

Linseed oil: Refined oil from flax seed used as a paint or glaze additive.

Luster: The amount of light reflected by a paint; sheen.

Matte: *See* Flat.

Mineral spirits: A petroleum-based solvent or thinner. Frequently sold as paint thinner or wood cleaner.

Native color: Inorganic pigment used to make an artist's oil paint. Used as a colorant.

Oil-based: Any interior paint containing an alkyd binder and paint-soluble thinner.

Paint: A spreadable emulsion of pigment, binder, and thinner.

Pigment: Finely ground organic and inorganic compounds that give paint its color.

Primer: A coarse underbody used to cover unpainted and previously painted surfaces so paint will adhere and cover more easily.

Resin: The viscous, pliant chemicals used as binders in paints. They hold the pigments in suspension.

Satin: A paint finish that has slightly more luster and reflectiveness than an eggshell finish, but less than a semigloss finish.

Scrubbable: The ability of paint to withstand repeated washings without losing its color or thickness. Also called washability.

Sealer: A coarse, nonabsorbent underbody used to seal porous or stained surfaces.

Semigloss: A hard, durable paint finish that has a medium amount of shine and light reflection.

Sheen: The amount of light reflected by a paint's finish, which results in its gloss.

Slip: The quality of a surface that doesn't permit paints and glazes to adhere to it easily; slickness.

Snap time: The point in time when a glaze has begun to dull down and become tacky.

Solvent: Anything capable of dissolving other substances.

Solvent-soluble: Capable of being dissolved in a petroleum solvent, linseed oil, turpentine, etc.

Tempera paint: Water-soluble paint made with pigment in an egg-oil emulsion. Used as a colorant.

Textured paint: Paint to which sand or other inorganic materials have been added to produce a texture on walls or other surfaces.

Thinner: Any liquid used to thin paint to a spreadable consistency. The most common thinners are water and petroleum solvents.

Tipping off: The practice of lifting the tip of a decorator brush's bristles away from the surface at the end of a stroke. This feathers in the stroke and creates a thin, blendable wet edge.

Tooth: A slightly coarse surface that aids a paint's ability to adhere to it.

Top coat: Durable, transparent finish coat.

Touch dry: The paint surface won't smear when lightly touched even though it is not thoroughly dry.

Turpentine: A thinner and solvent derived from pine trees.

Undercoat: A sealer or primer that's applied before the base coat.

Universal tint: Colorant used to custom-mix latex and alkyd paints and glazes.

Vinyl: A synthetic resin used as a binder in latex paint.

Volatile organic compounds: The petroleum solvents contained in paint. They evaporate into the air and promote air pollution. Also called "VOCs."

Wash: A sheer layer of highly diluted paint that's used to create decorative finishes.

Washability: See Scrubbable.

Water-soluble: A glaze or paint that is compatible with water.

Wet edge: A margin of wet paint or glaze bordering an unpainted section. Leaving a wet edge creates a seamless blend between sections of work.

Wet stage: The point in time when a painted or glazed surface is wet and can still be worked without risking damage to the finish.

CHAPTER 3

The collection of tools used to apply and manipulate paint includes brushes, rollers, cheesecloth, sponges, graining combs, and more. Of all these, brushes are by far the most important, especially when it comes to executing fine details. In fact, professional decorative painters often say that the brush determines the success of a job. Therefore, it's imperative that you select the right one for each project. Brushes come in many sizes and materials. Your best bet is to buy the highest quality you can afford. Because the brushes for the general application of paint wear out quickly, buy good-quality, moderately priced brushes for those jobs and save your money for the highly expensive specialty brushes required for techniques, which can cost from $10 to $200 or more each.

Brushes and Other Creative Tools

Brushes of many types and sizes are required for a complex job, such as this wall mural, which was painted by artists John Agnese and Frank Carballeira

Decorator Brushes

Basic decorator brushes, the kind designed for interior painting, come with natural or synthetic bristles. The type of bristle determines the kind of paint you use.

Natural-Bristle Brushes. Intended for use only with oil-based products, these brushes are made with either boar bristles, identified by the generic name *china bristles*, or a blend of boar bristles and ox hair. The blend makes a good varnish brush because its fine, flexible bristles don't leave brush marks. Natural-bristle brushes are generally more costly than the synthetic-bristle ones and so you may want to avoid using them with water-based products. Animal hair absorbs water making the bristles limp over time. High-quality natural-bristle brushes have excellent shape retention and natural flagging—a splitting of the bristle ends—that helps them hold more paint, ensuring smooth paint release and finish.

4-inch nylon and polyester-bristle brush

4-inch natural-bristle brush

3-inch natural-bristle brush

Blended Nylon and Polyester-Bristle Brushes. This combination produces a high-quality brush: The nylon provides durability and the polyester provides shape retention. Because neither fiber absorbs water, these brushes work equally well with all water-soluble and solvent-soluble products. They apply paint smoothly and evenly. Easy to clean, a blended-fiber brush can last for years with proper care.

Polyester-Bristle Brushes. These brushes have good shape retention and maintain stiffness in water-soluble paints, glazes, and top coats. They also work well with solvent-soluble products, apply paint smoothly and evenly, are easy to clean, and can last a long time with proper care.

Decorator-Brush Basics. Buy decorator brushes in sizes suitable to your job. An all-purpose collection should include 1½- to 2-½-inch-wide sash brushes for use on woodwork and windows; 2-inch-wide trim brushes for cutting in at corners, along ceiling lines, and around woodwork; 3-inch- and 2-inch-wide brushes exclusively for applying varnish and other clear top coats; disposable brushes, either inexpensive or older used brushes.

Use 3- and 3½-inch-wide brushes for painting, sealing, priming, and base-coating large flat surfaces, unless you prefer to use a roller. (See "Paint Rollers," on page 72.) Four-inch-wide brushes also work well for big, flat surfaces, but they're larger and heavier; some people find them uncomfortable to hold for any length of time.

Save varnish or top-coat brushes for these uses only, not to apply paint. The paint residue left after cleaning them is likely to bleed into your next top coat. These brushes must be kept very clean.

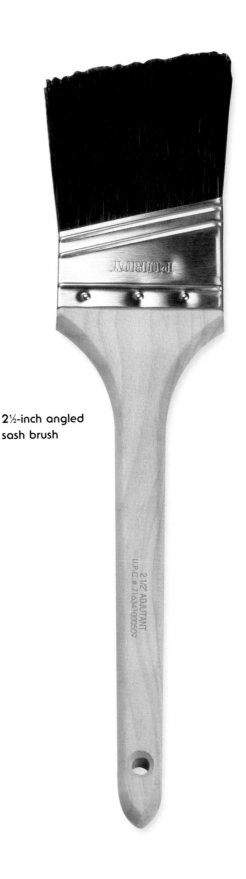

2½-inch angled
sash brush

6-part pipe grainer

Oval
sash brush

12-part
pipe grainer

Specialty Brushes

An astonishing variety of brushes designed specifically for use by artists and decorative painters is also made, both with animal hair and synthetic fiber bristles. The animal hairs include boar (or hog), ox, squirrel, horse, sable, camel, and badger. The same rules apply to these brushes as decorator brushes—use most animal-hair brushes with oil-based products; use synthetic-bristle brushes with either water-based or oil- and alkyd-based products. The following are the most useful specialty brushes:

- **Artist's brushes.** Soft- or stiff-bristled brushes used for applying and blending larger amounts of paint. Choose the bristle stiffness with which you're most comfortable. You need two or three sizes, ranging from a fine camel's hair brush to a wide, flat nylon brush with a pointed end to paint fine decorative details, including marbling effects and freehand work.

- **Blender brushes.** Used to blend and soften or grain all types of wet surfaces. Use badger-hair blenders, among the most expensive brushes available, with solvent-soluble products; use hog-hair blenders with water-soluble products.

- **Cutters.** Short, stiff-bristled brushes used to cut in lines

- **Dusting brushes.** Soft, medium-length bristle brushes used for dragging walls, stippling furniture and moldings, and softening glazes with texture.

- **Flogging Brushes/Draggers.** Wide, long-bristled brushes used to texture surfaces by dragging or slapping wet paint or glaze. They're useful for touching up mistakes.

- **Lining brushes.** Thin, flexible, long-bristled artists' brushes used for fine lining and other techniques. Using #0, #1, or #2 lining brushes gives you good control for painting intricate details.

- **Mottlers, also called spalters.** Flat-ended brushes used to make wood-like textures in glazed surfaces.

- **Overgrainers.** Long, flat-bristled brushes used in wood-graining techniques to put paint detail on dry, previously grained surfaces.

- **Pipe or pencil grainers.** Wide, hog-bristle brushes used to drag fine lines in paint or glaze and to create other effects.
- **Round fitches.** Round brushes with firm but flexible bristles used for spattering, stippling, and stenciling. They make a softer, more subtle stenciling effect than traditional stencil brushes.
- **Stencil brushes.** Round, short hog-hair brushes with blunt-cut ends used to pounce-on stencil paints and create other effects.
  - **Stipplers.** Blocky, stiff-bristled, hog-hair brushes used to stipple wet paints, glazes, and top coats.
  - **Toothbrushes.** Used for spattering. An inexpensive but highly effective tool.

All of these specialty brushes have bristles with the correct length, shape, and end flagging needed to do a specific job. How well they perform that job depends on their quality. Usually, the better the quality, the higher the price. A large stippler, for example, can cost more than $200. That's why professional decorative painters often use just a few of these brushes for special effects and develop most finishes with basic tools like rollers, decorator brushes, cheesecloth, and other common materials.

Flogging brush/dragger

2-inch flat oil brush

CONDITIONING NEW BRUSHES

Nothing is more frustrating than getting stray bristles in your wet paint. To prevent this, when you buy a new brush, no matter how expensive, remove any loose hairs. Wash the brushes in warm soapy water. Before they dry, move the bristles back and forth in your hand, and spin the brush between your palms so that any more loose bristles work their way into sight. Then just pick them out.

JUDGING BRUSH & ROLLER QUALITY

A quality brush has a sturdy hardwood handle; a tight metal ferrule around the neck where the handle joins the bristles; and thick, flexible bristles with split (flagged) or fuzzy ends. Decorator and varnish brushes have a tapered tip, which makes an even line when pressed against a flat surface. Above all, a quality brush should balance well in your hand. A roller's "cage" (which holds the sleeve or roller cover) should feel sturdy and have nylon bearings that spin smoothly. A high-quality roller will have a cage that is held securely without a wingnut.

Paint Rollers

It makes good economic sense to use a roller to apply sealers or primers, base coats, and some glazes to large surfaces. For very large surfaces, you can put the roller on an extension pole to maximize your reach.

Buy a quality roller made with a steel frame, nylon bearings, a wire sleeve, and closed ends. Sleeves come from 3 to 18 inches wide. Choose a width that gives you good coverage but doesn't overlap the edges of the space you're painting. A 9-inch-wide roller is standard for painting walls.

Also, choose the correct roller cover to suit the type of paint. Use a synthetic-fiber cover for water-based products; a wool, wool/nylon, or mohair cover for oil-based products. Foam roller covers also work well for applying oil-based glazes and top coats because they don't produce bubbles or leave brush marks.

Squeegee

Other Application Tools

It takes more than brushes to execute any decorative painting technique. With many techniques, you'll use tools other than a brush or a roller once the base coat is on. The most essential of these tools follow:

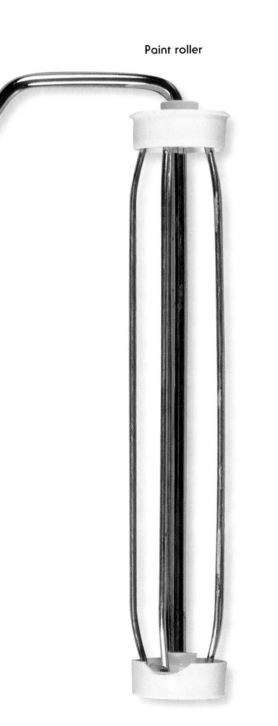

Paint roller

- **Broad knife.** For applying texturing compounds, to create stone textures like slate.

- **Chamois cloth.** Used to pick up paint thinner in negative spattering and to blend glazes in many other techniques.

- **Check rollers.** Used to make pore marks in oak wood graining.

- **Cheesecloth.** Used to create many different textures as well as to blend and smooth all techniques; a versatile and inexpensive tool. Also excellent for executing parchment or cloth-distressing techniques as well as for blending and off-loading glazes. Use 90-weight cheesecloth, available from craft shops and stores serving the painting trade.

- **Feathers, turkey or goose.** Used to make veins in marbling and other faux-stone looks. Turkey feathers are preferable because they are wider than goose feathers. They come in right and left orientations; choose the one that matches your hand orientation and your working angle.

- **Graining combs.** Flexible steel or plastic combs, which come in a variety of sizes, used to striate and grain surfaces. A common hair comb makes a workable substitute.

- **Natural sea sponges.** Used to apply random layers of paint over a base coat in techniques like sponging, color washing, and other techniques.

- **Old newspapers.** Used to off-load and blend glazes.

- **Rubber graining rollers.** Used to create a wood-grain pattern.

- **Rubber rockers or graining heels.** Used to create a heart-grain pattern in wood-graining techniques.

- **Squeegees.** Used to striate, drag, and comb surfaces. You can notch it yourself with scissors or a utility knife.

- **Steel wool.** Used to striate glazes and to create wood grain.

Other Tools of the Trade

These are the tools that make it possible for you to apply paint with a great degree of comfort and convenience. Among the most useful ones are

- **Buckets.** Disposable 1-quart 1-, 2-, and 5-gallon sizes for mixing and applying paints and glazes
- **Carbon paper.** For tracing stencils on acetate
- **Carpenter's level.** For laying out designs
- **Chalk-line box.** For laying out designs
- **Clean rags and old towels.** For cleaning up
- **Craft knife.** For cutting patterns in stencil acetate
- **Cutting board, padded.** For cutting stencils
- **Cutting glass.** Used in place of padded cutting board for cutting stencils
- **Disposable dishes or cups.** For mixing paint samples and small quantities of paint
- **Drop cloths, plastic sheeting, and old newspapers.** For protecting surfaces from paint splatters and spills
- **Fire extinguisher, household type.** For fighting possible small fires created by solvent fumes
- **Hand broom.** For giving surfaces a final dusting before painting
- **Jars.** For storing specialty brushes upright
- **Ladders, various types and sizes.** For easy access to all surfaces
- **Paintbrush comb.** For reshaping cleaned brushes
- **Painter's blue masking tape.** For protecting woodwork, defining areas to be painted, and anchoring stencils
- **Paint spinner.** For drying brushes
- **Paint tray.** For applying paint or glaze to a roller
- **Palette, disposable.** For mixing colors and for painting stencils
- **Palette knife.** For mixing paints and glazes
- **Paper towels.** For cleaning up
- **Pencil, #1 lead.** For tracing stencil patterns onto acetate or parchment
- **Rubber mallet or hammer and board.** For sealing can lids
- **Sanding block.** For holding sandpaper
- **Sandpaper.** For prepping surfaces and smoothing between coats, available in many grades
- **Scissors and utility knife.** For notching squeegees and making other cuts
- **Scrap cardboard or newspaper.** For off-loading excess paint from brushes
- **Stencil acetate or parchment.** For cutting stencil patterns
- **Stirring sticks, various sizes.** For mixing paints and glazes
- **Straightedge, metal.** For measuring and laying out designs
- **Tack cloth.** For cleaning up sanding dust
- **Toothbrush.** For cleaning tools
- **Vacuum cleaner or hand vac.** For cleaning up sanding dust

Tools and materials specific to preparing and repairing surfaces to be painted are discussed in Chapter 4, beginning on page 78.

Cleaning Your Painting Tools

All cleanup requires you to properly soak, rinse, and dry your tools, but the specific techniques for this task depend on the tool and the type of paint used. Here are some paint and tool-specific guidelines.

Brushes

Scrape excess paint onto the edge of a paint-mixing stick or corrugated cardboard, and then clean the brush with the appropriate solvent. Always finish with warm soap and water.

Latex Paint and Glaze. Wash the brush in warm, soapy water (dishwashing liquid works well) and rinse thoroughly. Shake it with a sharp, snapping motion to remove excess moisture. Comb through the bristles with a brush comb, and shape it with your hands. Hang a decorator brush by its handle to dry; stand specialty brushes on end in a jar. For long-term storage, wrap a brush in its original wrapper or newspaper once it is dry. Any dried paint can be scraped off with a wire brush or washed off with denatured alcohol.

Alkyd Paint and Glaze. Remove excess paint using a mixing stick, or brush it out on newspaper. Soak the brush in mineral spirits or turpentine; then work the solvent through the bristles. Repeat until the liquid is clear. Shake the cleaned brush, making a sharp, snapping motion with your wrist, and then wash it in warm, soapy water, rinsing it well. Comb the bristles with a brush comb; then twirl the brush inside a cardboard box or large pail. Shape the brush with your hands, and wrap it in its original wrapper or newspaper. Store a decorator brush by laying it flat or hanging it from its handle. Store a specialty brush by standing it brush end up in a jar. Put the dirty solvent in a can, and seal the lid; reuse it until it gets sticky. Once it's sticky, dispose of it as described on pages 60–61 of Chapter 2.

Brushes are an important investment—if you clean them properly, you can reuse them many times. Hang decorator brushes by their handles; store specialty brushes in a jar.

Rollers and Trays

Begin by scraping the roller cover over the edge of the paint tray, a paint bucket, a mixing stick, or a piece of corrugated cardboard to remove any excess paint. Pour the leftover paint into the can; then remove the roller cover from the roller and clean it with the appropriate solvent.

Latex Paint and Glaze. Flush the entire roller assembly under a strong stream of water until the water runs clear. Remove the cover, and wash it in warm, soapy water (dishwashing liquid works well); then rinse it until the water runs clear. Squeeze the excess water out of the cover with your hands, and roll it on a clean towel to remove as much moisture as possible. Stand the cover on end on another clean towel in an airy place to dry. When the roller is dry, wrap it in a clean towel or wrapping paper, and stand it on end to store. Never lay a roller cover on its side because it will flatten. Clean the roller carriage and the paint tray the same way, taking the carriage apart, if necessary. Dry the roller with a clean towel, reassemble it, and store it by hanging it in an airy place.

Alkyd Paint and Glaze. Soak the roller cover in mineral spirits or turpentine for several hours. Then, wearing latex gloves, work the solvent into the nap with your hands. Rinse the cover with fresh solvent until the liquid runs clear. Now roll the cover in a clean towel or newspaper to remove excess solvent, and then dry and store it as described above for cleaning latex paint from a roller cover. Use more solvent to clean the roller carriage and tray as described above for cleaning latex paint from a roller. Pour the cleaning solvent into a can, and dispose of it as explained in "Storing and Disposing of Paint," on pages 60–61.

Cleaning Other Tools

Follow the same directions given above: Wash the tools with soap and water or solvent (as appropriate), and hang or stand them up to dry. Simply swish feathers in solvent, and lay them out to dry. Use a toothbrush to scrub squeegees, check rollers, graining heels, and graining combs. Never leave a rubber tool sitting in solvent, because it will swell and become useless.

Personal Safety

Decorative painting seems like a benign project. Basically it is, but it involves the use of chemicals that can be harmful if they are not handled carefully or used correctly. Petroleum solvents can be hard on your skin and equally hard on your lungs if you breathe their fumes for too long. To protect yourself, follow these common-sense safety rules.

Always follow the manufacturer's instructions and safety precautions for using any product. This rule is sacrosanct. Never break it. This is especially important when you work with products containing petroleum solvents.

Always make sure your work area is well ventilated. Open all doors and windows in the work space to create good cross-ventilation. Use an exhaust fan if the area doesn't have good natural ventilation or if the air is still or humid. Also, turn off all sources of open flame in the area. Many paint products are combustible.

Keep the following personal safety items on hand. Use these items whenever you paint. You need them to protect yourself and your clothing against minor hazards, such as paint spatters, and more serious ones, such as having your skin come in contact with harsh solvents or breathing in their toxic fumes:

- **Dust mask and/or respirator.** To protect your nose and lungs from the fumes in solvent-soluble products. Wear a respirator when using any such products for a prolonged period or in a less than well-ventilated space.
- **Eye goggles or safety glasses.** To protect your eyes against paint spatters, dust, and the effects of fumes.
- **Latex gloves.** To protect your hands from caustic solvents and latex paint. Remember: Latex paint has a water base; it literally absorbs the moisture out of the skin, cuticles, and fingernails. If you're allergic to latex, wear a pair of cotton surgical gloves under the latex gloves.
- **Plastic bags, lawn size.** Use them to make big protective aprons you can wrap around yourself; tie them in place with strips of plastic bag.
- **Skin lotion.** Rub a rich lotion or petroleum jelly onto your hands, arms, face, neck, and other exposed areas before working to protect them from paint and solvent splatters.

Protect your skin, eyes, and lungs against the chemicals contained in paint products. Wear rubber gloves, goggles, and a mask when working.

Surface Preparation: Building Your Base

Professional decorative paint artists spend one to three hours preparing a surface for every hour they spend painting it. They do this because they know a decorative paint finish looks only as good as the surface to which it is applied.

Depending on the surface you plan to paint, preparation involves many tedious and messy steps, from washing walls and scraping paint to patching cracks and holes. All of these tasks are labor-intensive; that makes them tempting to skip. But a new coat of paint won't cover any flaws; it will only magnify them. Therefore, you should not avoid thorough preparation. You can make it go more quickly, however, if you use the right methods and tools.

Decorative finishes, such as glazing or stenciling, can add style to a bathroom. Before painting them, protect the walls against the assaults of moisture and mildew by building a base.

Tools for Preparing a Surface for Paint

The tools required for preparing a surface are generally project-specific. This list presents a number that come in handy for all types of jobs, from painting a small stool to covering all the walls and the ceiling of an entire room. Keeping your project in mind, review this list to determine your specific needs:

- **Broad knives** (6-, 8-, and 10-inch) to apply patching compounds, joint compounds, and wood putty.
- **Broom and dust mop** to clean before and after painting.
- **Brushes** (2- and 3-inch, disposable types) to apply chemical paint strippers and shellac.
- **Can opener** (punch type) to widen cracks in plaster.
- **C-clamps** (large) to secure planks used with ladders.
- **Double-backed tape** (2- or 3-inch) to hold drop cloths and plastic sheeting in place.
- **Drop cloths** to protect floors, carpets, and furniture.
- **Garden sprayer** (new or unused) to apply cleaning solutions and wallpaper remover.
- **Gloves** (latex, rubber, and surgical) to protect your hands.
- **Goggles or safety glasses** to protect your eyes.
- **Heat gun** (electric) to remove existing finishes from wood.
- **Knee pads** to protect your knees.
- **Ladders and planks** to reach difficult places.
- **Masking tape** (2-inch) to hold plastic sheeting in place.
- **Nail set and hammer** to reset nails on woodwork.
- **Nylon pot scrubbers** to remove greasy stains and

residue left by chemical paint strippers.
- **Orbital sander** to sand all types of surfaces.
- **Pails or buckets** to hold water, paints, and trash.
- **Paint scrapers** (hooked) to remove failing paint from woodwork and furniture.
- **Paint screen** to work paint into roller covers.
- **Painter's masking tape** (1½-inch) to protect woodwork and define areas to be or not to be painted.
- **Perforation tool** to break up vinyl coating on wallpaper.
- **Plastic bags** (30-gallon lawn bags with pull handles) to make protective aprons and dispose of trash.
- **Plastic bags** (15-gallon kitchen bags) to line trash baskets.
- **Plastic bags** (self-sealing 1-quart or sandwich-size) to store hardware items removed during preparation and painting.
- **Plastic sheeting** (2-mil thickness) to protect floors, carpets, and furniture.
- **Pole sander** (extendible) to sand hard-to-reach places.
- **Power screwdriver** to make repairs.
- **Putty knife** (2-inch) to apply patching compounds and wood putty to small holes and to remove chemical paint stripper.

- **Rags** to clean up.
- **Respirator** to protect your lungs from strong noxious fumes.
- **Roller covers** (disposable, ¼-inch nap) to apply paints and glazes.
- **Roller extension handle** to make rolling paint onto large surfaces easier.
- **Sanding block** to hold sandpaper.
- **Sanding screen** to smooth wallboard repairs.
- **Sandpaper** (various grits) to smooth surfaces and level repaired areas.
- **Screwdriver** to remove and reinstall hardware.
- **Sponge floor mops** to wash walls and floors.
- **Sponges** to wash and rinse surfaces.

- **Spray bottles** to apply cleaning solutions.
- **Steel wool** to remove chemical paint stripper.
- **Tack cloth** (commercially available sticky cloth) to clean up last of sanding debris.
- **Utility knife** for various cutting chores.
- **Vacuum** (hand size) to clean up sanding debris.
- **Vacuum cleaner with hand attachments** to pick up dust and sanding debris.
- **Wallboard saw** to cut wallboard for repair plugs.
- **Wallboard screws** (1¼-inch) to attach wallboard plugs and reattach wallboard to studs and joists.
- **Wire brushes** (brass, 2-mil, and fine bristles) to break vinyl coating on wallpaper and to remove failing dry paint.

80-grit sandpaper

Broad knife

Prepping Materials

The materials used in preparation work fall into three categories: removal chemicals, patching compounds, and sealers. Again, this master list presents materials needed for all types of projects, from small pieces of furniture to the walls and ceiling in a room. With your project in mind, review it to determine your specific needs.

Removal Chemicals

The following list of chemicals is project-specific. Not all of them will apply to your projects, but make sure you have what you'll need on hand before starting your work:

- Chemical paint strippers
- Commercial mildew remover
- Commercial wall cleaner or low-phosphate cleaner
- Commercial wallpaper remover (enzyme-based)
- Denatured alcohol to neutralize chemically stripped areas
- Liquid chlorine bleach to remove mold and mildew
- Liquid paint deglosser to dull semigloss and gloss surfaces
- Mineral spirits (white) to clean wood surfaces sealed with varnish or clear top coats
- White vinegar to neutralize surfaces washed with detergents or other cleaners
- Wood cleaner

LADDERS

You'll need to use ladders when you apply decorative paint finishes to a wall or ceiling. The right ladder is essential for efficiency—providing easy reach—as well as safety.

The best ladder arrangement consists of two 6-foot stepladders set 10 feet apart, their steps facing inward, with a 12-foot-long 2x10 plank positioned so that each end extends 1 foot beyond each ladder's steps. Secure the plank to the ladders with large C-clamps. This makes a sturdy, serviceable, yet easily moved scaffold that lets you work on ceilings and across broad expanses of wall without having to stretch beyond your normal reach and without having to stop every few strokes to move a free-standing ladder to a new position. It also lets you keep your paint and tools within easy reach.

To work in stairwells, run the plank from one ladder's steps to a stair. The plank should be level and close to the wall, and it should reach to the back of the stair tread and extend 1 foot beyond the ladder's step. Again, secure the plank to the ladder with C-clamps.

Patching Compounds

When your decorative paint project involves a wall or woodwork, you may have to make minor repairs to the surface beforehand. Here's what you'll need to patch holes or cracks in these surfaces:

- Acrylic caulk to seal seams between woodwork and walls
- Wallboard tape (either paper or self-adhesive fiberglass mesh) to repair damaged wallboard
- Joint compound to patch and seal damaged wallboard
- A latex bonding agent to secure plaster repairs
- Latex wood putty to repair defects in wood surfaces
- Patching plaster blended with latex bonding agent to repair defects in plaster surfaces
- White-pigmented shellac to seal repairs to damaged walls
- Window-glazing compound to seal seams between woodwork and walls

Sealers

In addition to patching compounds you may also need:

- Sanding sealers to fill open-grain wood before sanding
- Sealers to close surface pores in repaired spots
- Undercoats (either latex or alkyd) to prepare repaired surfaces to receive paint and give entire surfaces a consistent porosity

A light sanding *created a smooth surface on this folding screen before it was painted.*

REGARDING TEXTURED CEILINGS

Don't dust or wash a ceiling covered with textured acoustical spray. If the ceiling was sprayed before 1970, it probably contains asbestos and shouldn't be disturbed under any circumstances by a non-professional. Exposure to asbestos poses a serious health hazard. Options you may consider include covering the old ceiling with wallboard; floating a new ceiling; or hiring an asbestos abatement contractor to replace the ceiling.

Cleaning Surfaces

Washing all surfaces is an essential step before applying a decorative finish. Paint cannot bond to a dirty surface; to cover properly, it requires a surface that's free of all stains, dirt, grease, and dust. So after making repairs to a surface, clean it thoroughly.

To start, go over the surface with a vacuum cleaner, and then wash it with a commercial wall cleaner or a low-phosphate household solution. Spray the cleaner on the walls in a fine mist, working one section at a time. Let the solution stand for 5 minutes. Then, using a clean hand sponge for small surfaces or a clean sponge mop for walls and ceilings, scrub from the bottom up. Rub stubborn spots with a nylon pot scrubber or the mop's rough edge. *Note: These cleaners are caustic, so wear protection.*

Rinse the surfaces in the same order that you sprayed them, using a solution of ¼ cup of white vinegar in 1 gallon of water. Use a fresh gallon of rinse water and a clean sponge or mop for each wall. Let the washed surface dry overnight.

You may run into stubborn stains or situations that require special attention. Here are the typical culprits and a few special solutions for handling them.

Mold and Mildew. Although they look like splotches of dirt, mold and mildew are fungi that thrive in warm, damp rooms with poor ventilation. To get rid of them, scrub the surface using a hand sponge with a commercial mildew remover or a solution of 1 cup of chlorine bleach in 1 gallon of water. Let the solution set several minutes, and then rinse with the same vinegar-water solution used above. Allow the surface to dry overnight. Lightly sand the spot with 120-grit sandpaper, clean up the sanding dust, and seal the area with two coats of white-pigmented shellac. Allow the first coat of shellac to dry completely. Lightly sand it with 120-grit sandpaper, and clean up the sanding dust with a tack cloth before applying the second coat of shellac.

Grease Stains. If you have a grease-based stain that won't come off with ordinary washing, rub it with a little liquid deglosser. Allow the spot to dry overnight, and then seal it using the same method described under "Mold and Mildew," above.

Water and Rust Stains. These stains are signs of serious water damage. You'll have to eliminate the cause of the stains before correcting them, or they will appear again. When the area is completely dry, dig out and repair the damaged spots using the repair methods described under "Repairing Wallboard," "Repairing Damaged Plaster," or "Repairing Damaged Wood," pages 93–97. When done, wash and rinse the area the same way as you would unstained walls. Allow the area to dry overnight, and then seal it using the method described under "Mold and Mildew."

Before applying a wash to the kitchen cabinets, opposite, they had to be thoroughly cleaned. In a kitchen, grease can be a stubborn offender. If stains won't come off using a commercial cleanser or a vinegar-and-water solution, use a liquid deglosser.

Faux stone finishes may hide some flaws, but the surface must still be clean before work begins.

Semigloss or Gloss Finishes. After washing them as described under "Cleaning Surfaces," page 84, lightly sand them before applying a new finish. Use 150-grit sandpaper or a liquid deglosser applied with #00 steel wool if the gloss has a low or medium sheen. Apply the deglosser, following the manufacturer's directions. If the surface has a high sheen, sand it twice, first with 120-grit sandpaper, and then with 150-grit sandpaper or liquid deglosser and #0 steel wool. *Always wear latex gloves and eye protection when using deglosser.* Finish by rinsing the surfaces with a solution of ¼ cup of white vinegar in 1 gallon of water to remove the dust and neutralize the surface.

You can clean furniture and woodwork that is stained and sealed in much the same way; however, use mineral spirits or wood cleaner in place of water. Sand and degloss the surface the same way that is described under "Semigloss or Gloss Finishes," above.

Stripping Furniture and Woodwork

Three situations require you to completely strip off the existing finish from wood surfaces: thick layers of paint or varnish; large areas of damage; or the desire to change the finish completely. You'll have to get down to bare wood so you can start over. Accomplish this using one of three methods: dry scraping, working with an electric heat gun, or applying a chemical paint stripper. *If you are stripping paint that was applied before 1978, test it for lead, a hazardous substance, before trying to remove it.* You can purchase a test kit for this purpose from a hardware store. If lead is present, hire a professional for this part of the job.

Dry Scraping. This is the best method to use on a surface with only a few bad areas, especially if you plan to apply the same type of finish. The idea is to remove all the loose, damaged finish until you get to a smooth surface, but leave the undamaged finish intact.

With a hooked paint scraper and wire brush, scrape away all the loose paint. Work from the bottom up. Scrape well into the sound finish around each spot; although the paint may appear stable, it may be starting to pull away without showing. Follow this by sanding with 100-grit sandpaper to feather the edges of each spot into the existing paint. You need a final surface that's smooth and seamless to the touch. Make any necessary repairs to the surface. (See "Repairing Damaged Wood," pages 96–97.) End by sealing the surface with one coat of white-pigmented shellac if it's to be painted or with clear shellac if it's to be varnished. Let it dry overnight.

Electric Heat Gun. This tool softens paint or clear finish so it can be scraped away; however, it's not recommended because it

Start with clean, bare wood *for the most even finish on painted wood cabinets.*

A chemical paint stripper will bring wood down to its bare state. Do this before painting or refinishing.

can scorch the surface. Also, it's tedious and potentially dangerous—a heat gun can start a fire, and the process exposes you to noxious fumes. It may also leave paint embedded in the wood grain, which you then have to remove with a chemical paint stripper, adding an additional step to the process.

If you use a heat gun anyway, wear heavy leather work gloves, a respirator, and eye goggles, and follow the manufacturer's directions for how long and how close to hold the gun to the surface you're stripping. Never use a heat gun on wood that has been treated with a chemical paint stripper.

Chemical Paint Stripper. Using this product is the best way to remove all finish down to the bare wood. However, before you start, understand that while a paint stripper is highly effective, it's also highly caustic. Always wear protective gear—eye goggles, a respirator, a plastic apron, and latex gloves—when working with one. Professional painters often put on a pair of cloth surgical gloves, wet them down with water, and then slip on latex gloves to create a strong barrier against these caustic chemicals. Follow the manufacturer's directions for safe and effective use, and always work in a well-ventilated area.

A wood-grain finish rejuvenates a handsome old piece of furniture.

Start by using a disposable brush. Working in 1-foot-square sections, brush a thick coat of the stripper in one direction over the surface. Do not stroke the brush back and forth, which can limit its effectiveness. Let it stand for the recommended time plus 10 minutes. If it starts to dry, apply another coat. When the time is up, scrape off as much of the finish as possible using a #0 steel-wool pad, putty knife, or nylon pot scrubber. Change to a new steel-wool pad when one becomes too loaded to pick up more finish; rinse a pot scrubber or a putty knife in a bucket with 2 cups of white vinegar in 2 gallons of water.

When all the stripper has been removed, buff the surface with #0000 steel-wool and denatured alcohol to remove the last bits of finish and stripper and to neutralize the surface. Always rub with the grain of the wood. Let the surface dry at least 24 hours.

REMOVING TEXTURED PAINT

Cleaning textured paint from walls is a messy job, but it's not difficult if you follow this process. Mix a bottle of wallpaper remover that has reactive enzymes with 1 cup of white vinegar, 2 cups of liquid fabric softener, and 1 gallon of water. Pour this solution into a new (unused) garden sprayer. Start in one corner, and then work around the room in orderly sections, spraying each section with a fine mist. Work from the bottom up. Let the solution stand for 5 minutes. Spray again in the same order, and let it stand another 5 minutes; spray a third time, and let it stand another 5 minutes. Then, using a broad knife, scrape the texture, being careful not to mar the base surface. Using the remaining remover, wipe the walls with a sponge or sponge mop to pick up any residue. Rinse the entire surface with a solution of ¼ cup of white vinegar in 1 gallon of water. Let the surface dry, and then seal the walls with a coat of white pigmented shellac applied with a disposable brush or disposable roller cover.

Removing Wallpaper

Beside the obvious unsightliness, there are three reasons why you should remove wallpaper before applying a decorative finish:

- The covering may not be properly adhering to the wall
- Wet paint will loosen the adhesive underneath the wallpaper, which will then pull away from the wall
- Dyes in the wallpaper can bleed into the paint finish

A strippable paper that was correctly applied will pull away from the wall quite easily and cleanly. However, you may have to soften the paste residue with a sponge and hot water and scrape it away using a 6-inch broad knife. If the paper isn't strippable, a rented wallpaper steamer can help soften its adhesive so that it can be scraped away, but this method is cumbersome, messy, and time-consuming at best. Instead, do the job with a commercial wallpaper remover that contains reactive enzymes. You can find this product at a home-improvement center or paint store. When shopping, check the product label, which should state that the remover is enzyme-based. If it doesn't, find another that does.

Removing the wallpaper isn't difficult. Use a perforating tool (also called a scarifier) or 60-grit sandpaper to break the surface of a water-resistant or nonporous vinyl product. Do this so the remover can get to the adhesive behind the paper. Work in a circular motion, applying just enough pressure to score the surface. Pour 1 gallon of the remover into a new (unused) garden sprayer, and spray it on the walls in a fine mist. Work from the bottom up, one section at a time. When you've sprayed all the walls, repeat the process in the same order, then again a third time. Wait 15 minutes. After time is up, use a 6-inch broad knife to scrape each strip of wallpaper off the wall. Work from the bottom up and around the room in the same order as you sprayed the remover. Spray the bare walls with the remaining remover, and wipe them down using a clean hand sponge or sponge mop to remove all the adhesive residue. Rinse the walls with a solution of 1 cup of white vinegar in 1 gallon of water. Let the surface dry overnight.

Repairing Surfaces

All surface repairs include three basic steps: scraping, patching, and sanding. Rather than repeat all of the steps for these techniques with each specific repair presented in this chapter, they are presented just once for easy reference. Refer to them as necessary for making repairs to the surface of your project.

Use a special paper scraper or a broad knife to remove wallpaper. Afterward, make sure all adhesive residue is removed as well.

Scraping

Surfaces with peeling, chipped, or bubbling paint should be scraped before they are washed. Hold a paint scraper at a 45-degree angle, and drag or scrape it back and forth with firm pressure until the loose paint comes off and the area is completely clean. Be sure to work well into the paint around the damaged area because that paint may also be pulling away without showing. When all the loose paint is removed, sand the spots smooth and level using 120-grit sandpaper, clean up the dust, using a tack cloth, and seal the surface with a coat of white-pigmented shellac.

Patching

Except for tiny holes such as those made by a picture-hanging nail, patching is always done with perpendicular crisscross strokes. Apply the patching compound using a putty knife or a broad knife, as the flaw's size dictates. The tool should be wide enough to cover the width of the damaged area in one pass. Fill the void with the compound, working it into the defect with horizontal strokes. Begin at the bottom, and work to the top, making all the strokes in one direction. When the void is filled, immediately pull the tool down vertically across the damp compound to skim off any excess. If the flaw is small and shallow, the compound should fill the void at this point so that it's flush with the wall and feathered out onto the surrounding surface.

Repair any holes in the wall before applying any paint technique. Artist Lucianna Samu applied an antique finish to the walls of this dining room.

If the hole is deep and larger than ½ inch but still small, apply the compound in two layers to avoid shrinkage. Apply a thick first coat to within ⅛ inch of the surface, and let it dry overnight. Lightly sand with 120-grit sandpaper, clean up the dust, and skim the second coat over the patch. Let it dry overnight. Sand the patch with 120-grit sandpaper, clean up the dust, and seal the patch with white-pigmented shellac.

Sometimes defects require three patch coats. In this case, leave the first coat rough after it has dried. Skim the second coat over the first, and let it dry overnight. Lightly sand it with 120-grit sandpaper, clean up the dust, and skim the third coat over the patch. Complete the repair as described above.

Sanding

Sanding produces a slightly rough finish that helps paint bond with a surface. That's why it is important to take time to sand after each step in a repair. Most often, you can rub lightly, just enough to remove peaks of patching material and polish the surface without digging into it. However, the final sanding should feather the edges into the existing material.

Use a wallboard sanding screen, a hand-held sanding block, a pole sander, or an orbital palm sander for smoothing small repairs. Use a larger power sander for large repairs. Never use a belt sander because it can groove the surface. Sand wallboard and plaster along the longest direction of the repair, but always hand-sand wood with the grain. Wear a dust mask or, better yet, a respirator when sanding. Also, seal the room from the rest of the house as much as possible.

Repairing Wallboard

Although wallboard doesn't crack as easily and randomly as plaster, it does have problems with popped nails, dents, punched-in holes, and open joints. All are relatively easy to fix.

Popped Nails. Popped wallboard nails aren't a sign of poor construction; rather, they're the result of a home's normal expansion and contraction. To fix them, first drive 1¼-inch wallboard screws into the framing about 2 inches from each popped nail. Countersink the screws to ⅟₃₂ inch below the wallboard's surface. This should pull the wallboard tight against the house's framing; then remove the popped nail and scrape away any loose materials. Cover the nail hole and screw heads with premixed joint compound using the technique described under "Patching" on the previous page.

Sponging and ragging *techniques give these walls a textured appearance.*

Before adding a wood-grain finish *to an old mantel, all surface imperfections were mended.*

Shallow Dents. If the paper around a small dent's perimeter isn't broken, fill the dent with all-purpose interior joint compound, using the technique described under "Patching," page 92. If the paper is broken or the edges are cracked, cover the area with fiberglass mesh tape (preferred) or moistened paper joint tape, and apply joint compound as described under "Patching."

Large Holes. Large holes—anything larger than two inches wide—require a backing. Measure the hole's width and height. Cut a rectangular patch larger than the hole from scrap; center this patch over the hole and trace its outline onto the wall with a pencil. Use a wallboard saw to cut out the marked area.

Cut two or more backer strips out of 1x2 lumber, 3 or 4 inches longer than the hole. Slip them behind the opening, and attach them to the wall with 1¼-inch screws.

Large holes or open joints would ruin a delicate painted finish, such as a wall mural.

Push the patch into the opening, and secure it to the backer strips with 1¼-inch wallboard screws. Apply strips of self-adhesive fiberglass mesh tape or moistened paper joint tape to the patch's seams, overlapping the taped ends. Complete the repair as described under "Patching."

Open Joints. Stress cracks, which are hairline cracks in the wall, are hard to repair permanently because they tend to reappear when the house shifts. The most successful repair method involves filling such cracks with joint compound, applying fiberglass mesh tape, and adding a finish coat when dry.

If the crack is more than a hairline fissure but narrower than ¼ inch, widen it slightly, and undercut its sides using a utility knife. If the crack exceeds ¼ inch in width, leave it alone. Remove the loose debris from the crack with a vacuum or brush. Then, using a broad knife, work the joint compound into the crack and the surrounding area using the technique described under "Patching." Instead of sealing the patch with

white-pigmented shellac, reinforce the crack along its entire length with self-adhesive fiberglass mesh tape (preferred) or moistened paper joint tape. Apply three separate coats of joint compound over the tape, using the crisscross technique described under "Patching." Smooth the patch with sandpaper or a sanding screen after each coat, and end by sealing it with white-pigmented shellac.

Minor cracks will not mar a wall intended to look aged. These walls feature a subtle wash of color applied with a sponge.

Smooth wall surfaces *are especially important in a child's room. This playful mural enlivens a young girl's play space.*

Repairing Damaged Plaster

It's far too difficult for an amateur to attempt to repair large areas of damaged plaster. Hire a professional plasterer to do the job, or cover the entire wall with wallboard as described in "Floating Walls and Ceilings," page 98. However, you can repair small cracks and holes and other defects up to 12 inches square—but before you attempt any plaster repairs, do three things:

- Test the plaster around the defect for soundness. Scrape away any weakened areas, working outward until only a sound plaster surface remains around the defect's entire perimeter
- If the plaster is textured—most are—scrape off the texture around the defect. You will replace it when you paint
- Clean away any loosened material, and dust the hole with a clean brush. Then dampen the surface around the hole with a latex bonding agent following the manufacturer's directions

Filling Defects Under 3 Inches Square. Patch small holes and cracks by filling them with interior patching compound. Use the technique described under "Patching," page 92.

Filling Defects Up To 12 Inches Square. Use patching plaster for these repairs. Mix the plaster and water until you have a thick, smooth material. Patch as described under "Patching," page 92, adding this step: Let the first coat of patching plaster set for 15 minutes. Then, using a nail or knife, score it at ½-inch intervals in a crosshatch pattern. Mix the final coat of patching plaster with water until it's creamy. Apply this finish coat over the base coat, making it as smooth as possible. Let it set for 30 minutes to 1 hour. Then smooth the patch with a damp sponge—this will eliminate the additional step of sanding the patch. Let this final coat harden completely, and then seal it with a coat of white-pigmented shellac.

Repairing Damaged Wood

Always clean, repair, and sand a wood surface before applying any finish. You have already completed the first step in this process if you dry-scraped and smoothed the damaged spots or completely stripped the old finish.

If the wood has been scraped and sanded smooth, wash it as you would a wall, and *immediately* buff it completely dry with a soft towel. (See "Cleaning Surfaces," pages 84–86.) Don't let wet wooden surfaces air-dry. If the finish is semigloss or gloss enamel, wipe it down with a liquid deglosser and #0 steel wool, or lightly sand it with 150-grit sandpaper. If it has been stripped of all finish, you can skip these first two steps.

Apply latex wood putty to all damaged spots, following the manufacturer's directions. Let the putty dry for 24 hours; then sand the patched areas with 150-grit sandpaper, and seal them with white-pigmented shellac. In about an hour, when the shellac is dry, sand the entire area again with 150-grit sandpaper, and seal it with another coat of white-pigmented shellac.

Repairing Badly Damaged Walls

Sometimes walls are in such bad condition that ordinary repairs can't rescue them. This includes walls painted with textured paint and walls with many layers of paint, whether or not that paint is peeling. In these situations you have no choice to but to give the walls a new surface by smoothing them.

There are four ways to smooth walls and ceilings:
- Tear out the existing surface and hang new wallboard— a messy, expensive, and time-consuming process
- Glue and screw ¼-inch-thick sheets of new wallboard over the existing wall, which requires you to remove all the woodwork before you install the wallboard, and then reinstall it after the new wallboard is hung
- Float defective walls and ceilings with joint compound
- Strip off textured paint

Of the four, floating the walls is the most practical solution—it's also the only safe solution if your walls might have lead paint.

Wood putty *fixed minor damage to an antique mirror and table that's used as a vanity.*

Floating Walls and Ceilings. This is a quick, reliable, inexpensive, and fairly easy way to stabilize and seal a badly damaged wall. The technique, also called mudding or skim-coating, takes a few hours over three days to complete. It works well on all surfaces except those finished with textured paint.

Start by scraping the peeling paint with a broad knife or wire brush. Be careful not to mar the surface. Wear a respirator to protect your lungs from the dust. Then sand all the surfaces with a pole sander and 40-grit sandpaper. Vacuum the dust, and then damp-mop the entire area to pick up any residue.

Using a disposable brush or disposable roller cover, coat all the surfaces with white-pigmented shellac. Let them dry completely (about 1 hour). Then lightly sand with 100-grit sandpaper. Clean up the sanding dust, and apply a second coat of shellac. Let that dry completely, and then sand it with 120-grit sandpaper, and clean up the dust.

Thin premixed joint compound with water until it's the consistency of cake frosting. Visually divide the surfaces into 4-foot-square sections. Apply the compound to these sections in large, sweeping strokes, using a wide knife.

For walls, start in a corner on the lower half of the wall, and apply a thin layer of the compound to the first section, troweling it smooth. Then, working across the wall, repeat the process on each adjoining section until the lower half of the wall is covered. Return to the starting corner, and float the top half of the wall the same way. Repeat this with each wall. Let the compound dry overnight. The second day, lightly sand the surface with 120-grit sandpaper. Clean up the dust, and apply a second coat of joint compound the same way, smoothing as you work to reduce the amount of sanding needed. Let that dry overnight. On the third day, lightly sand with 120-grit sandpaper. Clean up the sanding dust. Finish by sealing all surfaces with a coat of oil-based sealer or white-pigmented shellac.

For a ceiling, use the same technique, starting in the corner at one end of the room. Cover the first row of 4-foot-square sections across the width of the room. Repeat the process until the ceiling is covered. Finish it the same way as for walls.

Building a Base

Now that you've demonstrated your commitment to your decorative painting project by taking the care—and time—to properly prepare the surface, you're ready to build the base on which you'll apply your chosen technique, through the use of primers or sealers and a base coat of paint.

Readying the Room

Prepare the room by removing as much furniture as possible before you apply the undercoat and base coat. Place any remaining furniture in the center of the room, and cover it with plastic sheeting and drop cloths for protection. Strip the walls of all light fixtures, electrical plates, register grilles, and anything else capable of interfering with a brush or a roller. Put small items, such as switch plates and screws, into small plastic bags and label them for safekeeping. If you're painting the ceiling, drop any light fixtures away from the ceiling surface, and cover them with plastic lawn bags.

When the room is cleared, vacuum the carpet or sweep the floor with a broom to remove any dust. (You don't want it to settle on your work surface.) Dust the baseboards, too. Run strips of 1½-inch-wide painter's masking tape along the edges of all trim, and cover the floor with drop cloths.

Before painting a ceiling, apply painter's masking tape to the walls at the ceiling line. If you're painting woodwork, apply the masking tape to the walls, butting it tightly against the woodwork and then attaching plastic sheeting to protect the walls' surfaces. For smaller projects such as painting furniture, set up a work area in a well-ventilated, well-lit space, and cover the surrounding area with plastic sheeting, drop cloths, or old newspapers. If you have a garage where you can work—with the door open—all the better.

Preparing a room for a large project, such as a mural, entails vacuuming, properly masking all woodwork, and removing all of the electrical plates, grilles, and registers.

PLANNING THE PAINTING SEQUENCE

Plan your working sequence before you begin. Professional painters usually paint a room in this order: ceiling, walls, window and door trim, doors, ceiling-line molding, baseboards, and floor.

Paint panel doors in this order, always brushing with any wood's grain, horizontal strokes on horizontal sections, vertical strokes on vertical sections: panels, center stiles (central vertical sections); top rail (top horizontal section); center rail (center horizontal section); bottom rail (bottom horizontal section); side stiles (side vertical sections); opening edge.

Notice that the top sections in each of these areas should be painted before the bottom sections. You should always work in the direction of your dominant hand. Divide flush doors into six sections and move the paintbrush in the direction of your dominant hand.

Prop furniture to be painted upside down on blocks on top of a large plastic sheet, drop cloth, or layers of old newspapers, and then paint from the bottom up. When the underside and sides are painted and dry, turn the furniture right side up, and paint the top.

Sealing and Priming

Always seal or prime a new surface. (See "Undercoats," page 45.) Undercoats come in three formulas: water-based (latex), alkyd-based (also known as oil-based), and alcohol-based (shellac). If you haven't selected your paint system, do so now because its formula influences the types of other products you'll apply over it. Remember: Both oil- and water-based products can be painted over water- or alcohol-based undercoats, but only oil-based products will properly adhere to an oil-based undercoat.

Most undercoats are white and add a subtle lightness to your base-coat color. Tint the undercoat to 50–75 percent of the base-coat color if that color is dark, deep, or very bright.

Undercoats come in exterior and interior grades; you'll need an interior-grade product, of course. They also come with additives that tailor them for specific jobs. A metal surface, for example, requires a primer, but whether or not that primer should also be rust-inhibiting depends on the metal. Iron needs a rust-inhibiting primer; aluminum does not. If you have any questions about the primer required for a surface you are finishing, talk to a sales professional at your paint store.

For your safety, always wear a mask when working with oil- and alcohol-based undercoats. They emit potentially harmful fumes that can make you feel sick and possibly do serious damage to your health. Keep the work area well ventilated.

Apply an undercoat with a roller the same way you do a base coat, but eliminate the laying-off strokes. (See "Painting with a Roller," page 102.)

Base Coating

At last, you're ready to start creating your decorative finish, which means you're about to capitalize on all your careful preparation work. By now you've decided on the look you want to render and the colors and products you want to use to execute it. Take time to make a sample of the finish, and study the sample in various lights in different parts of the room. (See "Making Sample Boards," page 112.) Examine it critically, and review your overall plan. Make any adjustments before you take another step. From here on, changing your mind will cause confusion, frustration, and extra expense.

It's wise to use a custom-mixed paint for your base coat. If you wish to mix your own color, follow the guidelines in Chapter 5, pages 114–115. If the base coat requires several gallons of paint, pour all of them into a 5-gallon bucket, and mix thoroughly to eliminate minor color differences between containers. This process is called *boxing*. Pour the boxed paint back into the cans, reseal them, and set them aside until needed.

You can use a brush to apply a base coat to small surfaces, but use a roller for large surfaces. A large surface is defined as an area or object that's larger than a set of double doors.

Painting with a Decorator Brush. Hold the brush lightly with your thumb supporting the underside of the ferrule (metal neck piece) and your first three fingers guiding it steadily from the top.

Glazed walls in this kitchen display even, uninterrupted color partly because all of the base-coat color was mixed at one time.

Plan to paint in 4- to 6-foot-wide sections, with the paint for each section slightly overlapping that of the previous one. Use vertical strokes on walls and ceiling; work with the grain on woodwork and furniture.

Dip the bottom third of the brush's bristles straight down into the paint. Lift the brush straight up and slap it lightly against the inside of the pail or bucket. Never drag the bristles across the rim of the pail; this causes the bristles to wear and clump, and it floods the can's rim with excess paint that dries, cakes up, and causes a mess when you open and close the can.

Holding the brush at a 45-degree angle to the surface, apply the paint in a long, even stroke, slightly overlapping the end of the previous one. Spread the paint over an area, and then pull it into the next unpainted one. Touch the surface with the entire tip of the brush as you move along, and apply just enough pressure to flex the bristles and distribute the paint. As you end the stroke, feather the paint edges with the tips of the bristles by lifting the brush away from the surface while still moving through the stroke. This is called *tipping off*; it makes the paint as thin as possible on the wet edge so it blends with the first paint stroke that's applied to the next section.

Painting with a Roller. A roller is the best tool to use when painting large, flat areas because it spreads paint quickly and easily. Prime the roller to receive paint by thoroughly wetting the cover and then running it over a clean towel until it's dry; wet it with water if you're using a latex base coat or mineral spirits for an alkyd base coat. This wetting and drying process also removes any lint that's in the cover.

Divide the surface into 6-foot-wide, floor-to-ceiling sections. Fill the paint tray about halfway with paint. Use a 3-inch brush, cut in the base coat at the corner, along the ceiling line and baseboard, and around any other woodwork in the first section.

Hold a decorator brush *at a 45-degree angle to paint surfaces such as cabinets and doors.*

Dip the roller fully into the paint. Lift it from the tray, and roll it over a paint screen or the tray's ribbed area to work the paint into the nap. The roller should be full but not dripping.

Start at the bottom on the left-hand edge of the first section. Run the roller up to the top of the section in one long, steady stroke. At the top, immediately pull the roller down to the bottom at a 45-degree angle and back up to the top at another 45-degree angle to make the center of an M. Then pull the roller straight down from the top to the bottom to make the M's final stroke. Continue making overlapping Ms until the entire section is filled with paint. Reload the roller three or four times during this process.

For a seamless appearance, *blend wet paint from one section onto the next.*

Finish the section with a series of light strokes to smooth the paint in one direction. This is called *laying off*. To do this, pull the roller down from the top of the section to the bottom, lifting it away from the wall as you reach the end of the stroke. Return to the top and, overlapping the first stroke by 1 inch, pull the roller down the wall again. Repeat the process until the entire section is smoothed.

Work quickly so that the paint bordering the next section doesn't dry. This is called *leaving a wet edge*. This margin of wet paint lets you blend the paint into the next section so that you get a seamless appearance.

Applying a Top Coat

Make sure you have a painted surface that is thoroughly dry and completely free of dirt and grease before you apply a top coat. Painting a clear finish over a damp or dirty surface will cause it to craze and crack over time—if it doesn't bubble or bead up as soon as you apply it. If you're applying polyurethane, use a new can—these products deteriorate quickly once exposed to the air.

Apply your top coat with a roller (foam or fabric, as desired) or a brush reserved for varnishing. Apply three thin coats, letting each dry thoroughly before applying the next. Dilute the first coat by 20 percent, the second by 10 percent. After the second coat, lightly sand the area with 600- or 800-grit sandpaper. Clean up the dust, and apply the third coat full strength.

SURFACE PREPARATION

MATERIAL	Unpainted wallboard (new walls, ceilings)	Painted wallboard (existing walls, ceiling)	Unpainted plaster (probably new surface or architectural ornamentation)	Painted plaster (probably old surface or architectural ornamentation)	Raw or bare new wood or stripped old wood
CLEANING	Dust with a hand broom or a vacuum's soft brush attachment	Dust, wash with household cleaner, rinse with vinegar and water, dry overnight	Dust with a soft-bristled brush; sand smooth, if necessary. Clean up dust	Wash with household cleaner; rinse with vinegar and water solution; let dry for 48 hours	Lightly dust with a soft broom or a vacuum's soft brush attachment
PREPARATION	Patch with joint compound, if necessary. (See "Repairing Wallboard," pp. 93–95.) Spot-seal patches with white-pigmented shellac. Undercoat with latex primer or polyvinyl acetate (PVA) sealer	Patch with joint compound, or float, if necessary. (See "Repairing Wallboard," pp. 93–95 and "Floating Walls and Ceilings," p. 98.) Spot-seal patches with white-pigmented shellac. Prime with latex or alkyd primer if existing paint is worn or strongly colored	Repair flaws with joint compound or patching plaster. (See "Repairing Damaged Plaster," p. 96.) Spot-seal with white-pigmented shellac. Prime with alkyd (preferred) or latex primer	Repair flaws with joint compound or patching plaster. (See "Repairing Damaged Plaster," p. 96.) Spot-seal with white-pigmented shellac. Prime with alkyd or latex primer, if needed	Seal knots with white-pigmented shellac; repair damaged spots with latex wood putty; caulk seams as needed. (See "Repairing Damaged Wood," pp. 96–97.) Spot-prime as needed with white-pigmented shellac. Apply oil-based enamel sealer if surface is to be painted, sanding sealer if it's to have a clear finish. Let dry; lightly sand; clean up dust
BASE COAT	Latex or alkyd paint	Alkyd or latex paint, depending on primer	Alkyd preferred, latex acceptable	Alkyd or latex paint, depending on type of primer	Alkyd paint

AT A GLANCE

Painted wood	Laminates, plastics, resins	Aged unglazed masonry (If new, age six months before painting)	Corrodible metals	Noncorrodible metals
Wash with household cleaner; rinse with vinegar and water solution; wipe dry with towel, or wipe down with mineral spirits and air dry. Let stand 24 hours	Wash with household cleaner; rinse with vinegar and water solution; dry overnight. Wipe down with denatured alcohol	Scrub the surface with a wire brush and strong detergent; rinse with vinegar and water solution. Scrub again with water and muriatic acid solution; rinse; wipe dry; let stand overnight	Remove rust with a wire brush; clean up dust; wash with household cleaner; rinse with vinegar and water solution; wipe dry; let stand overnight	Wash with household cleaner; rinse with vinegar and water solution; wipe dry; let stand overnight
Scrape away loose paint; fill damaged spots with latex wood putty; degloss as needed. (See "Repairing Damaged Wood," pp. 96–97.) Spot-seal with white-pigmented shellac. Apply an alkyd (preferred) or latex primer	Roughen surface with sandpaper, followed by wipe-down with liquid deglosser or acetone. Apply alkyd or plastic-guard primer	Repair flaws with patching cement or mortar, if needed, and apply alkyd or latex sealer	Roughen surface with sandpaper, followed by wipe-down with liquid deglosser. Apply an enamel primer that contains rust inhibitors	Sand, working in a circular motion, or rub down with liquid deglosser
Alkyd or latex paint, depending on primer	Alkyd paint	Alkyd or latex paint depending on sealer	Alkyd enamel paint	Alkyd paint or appliance epoxy

You've reached the point where you're ready to mix your own paint and glaze colors. You're also about to discover one of decorative painting's rewards: the satisfaction of making paint and glaze to your own exact specifications.

Mixing Paints and Glazes

As previously mentioned, it's possible to create a handsome finish with custom-mixed paints selected from a manufacturer's color-chip system. You may want to stick to this, especially if you are a true beginner—these custom-mixed paints come in an infinite number of consistent colors, which makes them easy, convenient, and economical to use for base coats and glazes. Still, nothing beats the satisfaction of creating your own paints and glazes to achieve the subtleties in color and the individuality that decorative painting brings to your home.

A custom-mixed glaze was used to produce the perfect color in this kitchen. The skill involved in the mixing process comes with practice.

This chapter shows you the steps to follow to create your own colors, but there is really only one way to develop consummate skill at this task, and that is by doing. As with everything else, experience is the best teacher. The more you practice, the more you'll learn about color, its values, intensities, and proportions, and how they influence one another. You can never know too much about this complex subject. But in no time at all you'll develop an instinct for how much of each hue you'll need to create the exact color you want for your project's base coat or glaze. Just keep experimenting with various colors until you come up with right mixture.

The Basic Color Palette

There are 14 basic colors you can use to produce almost any hue you need. There are additional colors, of course—well over 500, if you take into account all the different artist's media around the world. However, these 14 are the most common, and their names are standard in all the media used to create decorative paint finishes: universal tints, artist's acrylics and oil paints, and japan colors. Start with these 14 and add others as the number and complexity of your projects grow.

The 14 Basic Colors

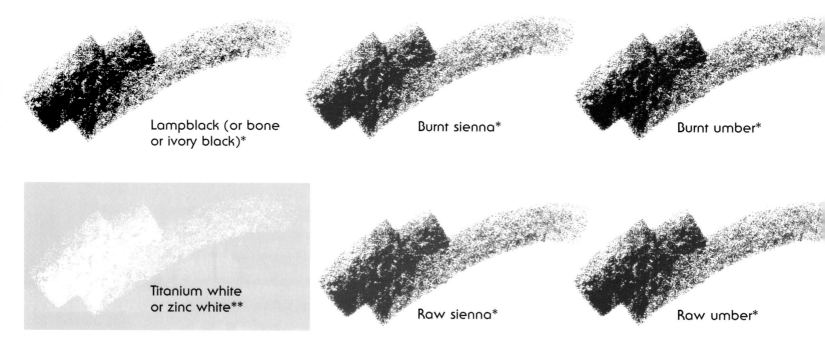

Lampblack (or bone or ivory black)*

Burnt sienna*

Burnt umber*

Titanium white or zinc white**

Raw sienna*

Raw umber*

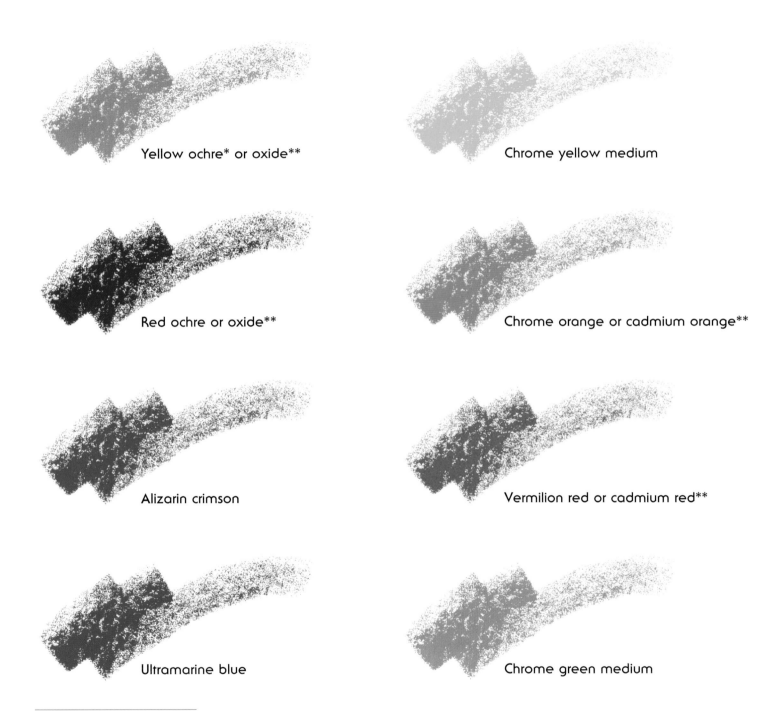

Yellow ochre* or oxide**

Chrome yellow medium

Red ochre or oxide**

Chrome orange or cadmium orange**

Alizarin crimson

Vermilion red or cadmium red**

Ultramarine blue

Chrome green medium

*These are the basic native colors that give you great control in neutralizing or toning down colors. (See "Intensity," page 25.)

**Basically the same color; the pigment listed first is the less expensive of the two.

Note that all these colors have medium values. It's most economical to use medium values because these can be used in a number of projects, as they are easier to either lighten or darken with a dollop of additional paint.

Paints

The Paint Mixer's Art

Like great cooks who use taste experience to add a little of this and a dash of that to create delicious meals, professional decorative painters use their eyes to estimate the amount of each colorant they need to achieve a specific tint or shade. With practice, you'll learn to do the same. Don't worry about measuring; mix your paint on a palette, adding colorant or glaze drop by drop, watching how the hue develops as you go. Increase the color very slowly, because all of a sudden it will be exactly what you want. One drop too much, and you've gone too far. But in no time, you'll discover and remember how much of each color it takes to achieve the results you want. Eventually you'll have enough skill and judgment to add all the colorant at once.

As you work, keep a thorough record for each project, noting how many drops of each colorant you use to make each color. Also, make a sample board of the final colors. Label any cans of leftover paint and the sample board with the project's name and the number of drops of each colorant used. This makes it possible for you to find the same paint when you need to use it for touch-ups. It also makes it possible for you to reproduce the color in the future. You'll find it easier to keep accurate records if you develop a system for abbreviating colorant names. Industry abbreviations for concentrated colors often involve numbers as well as initials and get quite complicated. Develop your own system, and keep it simple. For example, LB for lampblack, BU for burnt umber, and so on.

The more you practice, the more you'll learn how colors respond when combined. You'll notice, for example, that there are slight variations among different brands of colorants with the same name. You'll learn to account for those differences. You'll also discover that it takes very little of some colors to produce bright or deep hues and a lot of other colors to achieve the same end. Several drops of blue, for example, will alter a base quickly and easily, whereas it takes much more yellow to achieve a similar impact.

PIGMENT SAFETY

A number of these pigments are considered toxic and must be handled with great caution. Poisoning can occur if paints with these pigments are inhaled or ingested. Highly toxic pigments include raw and burnt umber; cadmium red and orange; chrome green, yellow, and orange; and vermilion red. Alizarin crimson, lampblack, and zinc white are considered slightly toxic. When working with these paints, avoid eating, drinking, or smoking; use a dust-mist respirator when sanding or mixing dry pigments; and never use household containers or utensils to mix paints.

REDUCING INTENSITY WITH NATIVE COLORS

Name: Yellow ochre

Color: Medium dull yellow

Effects: Reduces intensity of true yellow; neutralizes purple and red-purple; adds yellow to and dulls the intensity of greens; turns black green; warms other colors.

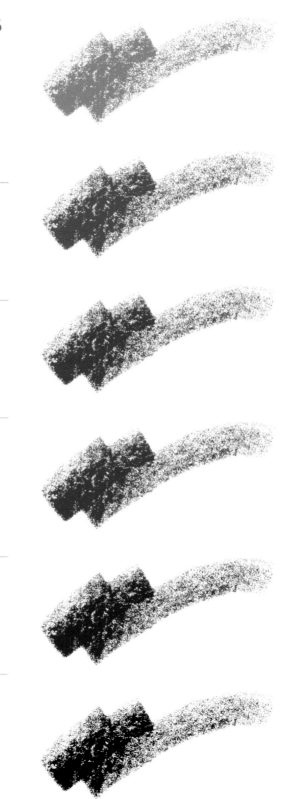

Name: Raw sienna

Color: Medium dull yellow-orange

Effects: Adds pink orange to colors, including white; dulls the intensity of yellow; neutralizes blue and violet.

Name: Burnt sienna

Color: Dark red-orange

Effects: Neutralizes blue, blue-green, and green; gives other colors a warm red-orange cast.

Name: Raw umber

Color: Dark-value green-based gray/brown

Effects: Turns most colors grayer and darker; neutralizes red-violet and red; adds green to other colors; makes good grays when mixed with black and white.

Name: Burnt umber

Color: Dark reddish brown

Effects: Neutralizes blue; makes warm grays when combined with black and white; turns other colors warm and dark.

Name: Lampblack

Color: Darkest value native color; contains blue; a cool color

Effects: Cools and darkens all colors; neutralizes orange, red-orange, and yellow-orange.

Referring to the lessons in "Intensity," on page 25, you can lower a too-bright color's intensity by adding a little complementary color or native color. Use black only as a last resort. It's true that adding black subdues a color's intensity, but it can also make it muddy and dull.

Each time you do a project, take a little extra time to experiment with small amounts of the leftover paint using the color's complementaries, split complementaries, and native colors to reduce its intensity. Do the same with white and black to alter its value. Take a bright blue, for example, and see what happens when you add a little orange, its complement; a little red-orange and yellow-orange, its split complementaries; and a little burnt sienna. Burnt sienna is a darker value red-orange; it lowers the blue's chroma, or intensity, every bit as successfully as the complementary and split-complementary colors, and it gives you a much broader range of complex, interesting colors in the process.

MAKING SAMPLE BOARDS

Make sample boards out of ⅛-inch-thick tempered hardboard that is smooth on both sides. An 18x24-inch board or a 24-inch square board is a good, workable-size surface. Prime the front of the board with the same primer you plan to use on the surface that will receive the decorative finish. When it's dry, apply the base coat. When that's dry, mark the back of the board with all pertinent information, including the number of drops of each colorant used to create the base coat's color. Now you have a sample board for that color. Over time, you will build an entire library of color sample boards.

There are two ways to make sample boards of specific decorative techniques. One is to take one board and layer the steps, one on top of another, until it displays the finished technique. Keep a careful record of what you do for each step in the process.

The other is to make a board for each step in the technique, starting with the base coat. Prime and apply a base coat to each board. Save one board for the base-coat sample. Then, just like a game of solitaire, work the first step in the technique on each remaining board, move to the third board, and work the second step on each remaining board, and so on until the final board shows the completed technique. Again, keep a careful record of what you do for each step, writing it on the back of each board. (See the opposite page.)

Because you're starting with a base coat, follow the 20-percent rule. This rule says that a colorant constitutes no more than 10 to 20 percent of a white or off-white base coat. If you need more than 20 percent of a colorant to achieve the desired color, buy a custom-mixed paint in a color close to the one you're trying to make, and adjust it slightly. For example, you'll find it impossible to mix a true red, a true yellow, or a true blue in a white base coat using the 20-percent rule; it takes far more colorant than that to achieve that end. That's why it makes more sense to buy a custom-mixed red, yellow, or blue base coat and adjust that to the exact intensity you want for your project.

All of these principles apply to mixing glazes, too, but because your medium is different, it calls for some adjustment. The difference is that glazes are translucent. As a result, you need very little colorant to achieve the right hue. The rule of thumb for glazes is to add one part color for a translucent glaze but less than one part color for a transparent glaze. As an example, just two or three drops of colorant will probably give you the color you want for a transparent color-wash glaze.

Ask your art supply dealer for a color-mixing chart; it usually contains useful technical information about permanence, translucence, and cost. Translucency ratings are important because they tell you which colors make a transparent glaze.

Also consider cost. Cost is directly related to quality, which comes in several grades. Because paint is usually a small part of a project's total budget, it makes economic sense to buy the best-quality product you can afford. Different colors in the same grade can carry different prices. The color-mixing charts indicate the substitution of effective cost-saving alternatives, such as using chrome yellow for cadmium yellow.

Bathroom Sponging

1. Randomly sponge on first glaze— cover 30% of base coat.

2. Apply second glaze to areas untouched by step 1.

3. Fill in additional untouched areas with third glaze.

Sample boards *with instructions for a technique make a handy reference.*

Mixing a Base Coat

Most base coats are a light or pale color. They usually consist of 80 to 90 percent white paint, with the colorant or colorants making up the balance. Part of the secret to achieving the right base-coat color lies in choosing the correct shade of white. Most paint manufacturers make it in at least three colorations, which are usually cool white, pure white, and warm white. Many manufacturers make far more whites than that. One actually offers 61 versions of white in its color-chip system. Choose your white base coat according to the warmth, coolness, or purity of the final color you want.

Follow these mixing guidelines, whether your base coat is a latex or alkyd paint:

For a small amount—less than 1 gallon, which is enough to cover a chair, for example—buy the quantity of white paint needed, and pour a cupful into a small container. Tint it to the desired color. As you work, make a careful record of the colorants and quantities so that you can reproduce the color later. Paint your sample, and blow it dry with an electric hair dryer. If the color is right once it dries, pour the remaining base-coat paint into another container, refer to your formula, and tint the remainder to the desired color. If the color is incorrect, play with your formula until you get what you want.

For a large amount—enough to base-coat an entire room, for example, which will take several gallons—

1 Fill a small container halfway with the base coat, directly from the can.

2 Tint the paint with the appropriate colorant. (See the table opposite.) Add the colorant directly into the paint, one drop at a time. Using a stirring stick or palette knife, stir the mixture well after adding each drop so that the colorant is completely diffused throughout the paint. After each thorough blending, make a small sample, and dry it with a hair dryer to test the color. Keep in mind that latex paint will look darker once it dries; alkyd paint looks about the same wet or dry.

3 *Keep adding, adjusting, and mixing until you have the desired result; then make a sample board, and label it with your formula. Keep the formula in your record book, too. Then use the formula to mix your large batch of paint.*

make the job simpler by buying one pint of white paint and pouring it into a small container, tinting it to the desired color. Keep a careful record of your formula. Make a small sample of the color, and use it to find a close match in a paint manufacturer's color-chip system. You may get lucky and find an exact match. If not, don't worry about it. Get as close as you can because you can adjust the color at home. Let the paint store custom-mix as many gallons of this color as you need.

If this custom-mixed base coat needs adjustment, pour one cup of it into a small container (Step 1). Using your colorants, refine the base coat to the exact color you want (Step 2). Mix it thoroughly (Step 3). Keep a careful record of the colorants and quantities that have been added.

Pour all the cans of paint into 1 large container. Following your formula, adjust the color with the colorants to match your sample. Add the 1 cup sample to this master mixture, and blend them thoroughly. When you get the color you want, pour it back into the cans, and seal them tightly by tapping around the lids' edges with a rubber mallet or hammer and board.

To keep paint from getting trapped in the rims of the cans, punch small holes in the bottom of the rim grooves before refilling the cans. After they're refilled, wait a few minutes while the paint in the rims drains through the holes into the cans before sealing the lids.

COLOR MIXING

TYPE OF PAINT	TYPE OF COLORANT
Latex base coat	Custom-mixed latex
	Artist's acrylics
	Universal tints
	(about 10%)
	Casein or tempera
Alkyd base coat	Custom-mixed alkyd
	Universal tints
	(about 10%)
	Artist's oils
	Japan colors

Washes and Glazes

Mixing a Wash

To make a wash, use the mixing steps described on pages 114–115, and dilute colored latex paint or artist's acrylics with water. The basic formula is one part colorant to two parts water; however, water can make up as much as 90 percent of the mixture.

Mixing a Glaze

All glazes are based on this basic formula: equal parts colorant, glazing medium, and appropriate thinner. The colorant may contain various amounts of several hues to achieve a desired result, but the combined total of these hues never exceeds the amount of colorant required by the formula. Specific glaze formulas appear with the instructions for each technique in "The Decorative Painting Techniques," Chapters 6 through 15, beginning on page 125. Always review the formula for a specific technique before you begin to prepare the glaze.

Remember, each formula is a guide, not an absolute. Like a recipe you adapt to your taste preferences and cooking style, you can adjust a given formula to achieve the amount of translucence and thickness you want. The rule of thumb is that the thinner—whether a water- or oil-based solvent—is the variable in a glaze formula. The amounts of colorant and glazing medium are usually equal. As with everything else in life, however, there are exceptions to this rule. These are noted in each technique's formula, as appropriate.

Once you mix the glaze, test its coherence. It should have the consistency of milk and resist flowing off the blade of a palette knife that has been dipped into it, pulled out, and then held at a 45-degree angle. Also test the glaze on a sample board painted with the base coat. You need only one sample board for testing. If the glaze doesn't have enough viscosity, wipe it off with a clean cloth, and adjust it accordingly. If necessary, wipe the sample board's surface with another clean cloth dampened with water or mineral spirits.

You'll have two big challenges to overcome when mixing a glaze: achieving the right amount of translucence and getting the correct viscosity or thickness. Glaze is a classic example of the less-is-more theory: You need a small amount of paint or colorant to color a glaze. The less color you add, the more transparent the glaze.

Mixing a glaze usually works best if you get the color right first, then mix it with the glazing medium and blend the combined colorant/glaze mixture with the thinner. Glazes have a fairly short shelf life, about ten days. If you want to keep the glaze longer than that, stop after blending the colorant and glazing medium; store this mixture in a tightly sealed container. Add the thinner only when you're ready to use the finished glaze mixture.

To make your glaze more translucent, try one of these methods:
- For a slight change, add more thinner, but be careful not to add too much and make the glaze too thin
- For a dramatic change, add more glaze medium and more thinner in the same ratio you used for the original glaze
- Mix a new glaze using less colorant

To thin a too-thick glaze, add more thinner, a little at a time so you don't go overboard. A runny glaze is a difficult medium to work with, especially on a vertical surface. Keep thinning and testing until you get the exact consistency you want.

Thickening a too-thin glaze is much more difficult. Simply starting over is usually best, but if this involves a large amount of glaze that you don't want to waste, let it stand uncovered until some of the thinner evaporates. This may take 12 hours or more. If a skin forms on top of the glaze, strain the mixture through cheesecloth.

The marketplace offers many premixed glazing media. You'll find that they vary widely in both viscosity and translucence. Experiment with all of them, and then pick the brand that gives you the results you're after.

Mixing a Latex Glaze

In a clean container, mix your colorant with a transparent acrylic or latex glazing medium. Use custom-mixed colored latex paint, universal tints, or artist's acrylics for your colorant, as you prefer. When it's thoroughly blended, transfer this mixture to a larger container, and slowly add water until you get the desired consistency. As an alternative, when mixing large amounts, add your colorant directly to the container of glaze medium and mix them thoroughly. Then pour the colored medium into a large container, and slowly add water until you achieve the correct thickness.

Whatever method you use to mix the glaze, keep testing it on your sample board, and keep adjusting it until you are satisfied. Always cover the glaze, and note the formula in your record book. If you're concerned about the glaze drying too quickly, add a retardant just before applying.

A colorant must be thoroughly blended with the glazing medium. Before glazing this wall, artist Lucianna Samu tested the color, and then adjusted it until it was perfect.

1 Lay the palette on a stable, flat surface. Place a dollop of the colorant at the edge. If the colorant consists of more than one hue, put dollops of the various colorants around the edges, as shown. Put the transparent glaze medium in the center of the palette. If you're mixing color for a large amount of glaze, omit the glaze medium.

MIXING ON A PALETTE

Some decorative painters like to use a palette to blend the colorant with the glazing medium. They also use this method to mix several colorants in order to produce the hue for a large batch of glaze. Follow the steps, opposite and below, for this technique.

FORMULA

BASIC LATEX GLAZE

- 1 part custom-mixed colored latex paint, artist's acrylics, or universal tints mixed into white latex paint

- 1 part acrylic gel medium or latex glazing liquid

- 1 part water

2 Spread the colorant or colorants toward the medium, mixing the ingredients with a palette knife to achieve the right color. Make it a little darker than the final hue you want, because adding thinner will lighten it. If you're mixing the color for a large amount of glaze, simply mix the hues together, and then blend with the glaze medium.

3 Scrape the colored glaze medium from the palette into a container. Slowly add thinner, stirring well after each addition, until you get the desired thickness. Cover the container, and shake it well. Test the glaze on your sample board. Keep adjusting it until you're satisfied. Cover the glaze, and note the formula in your record book.

Mixing an Oil Glaze

To make an oil glaze, blend custom-mixed colored alkyd paint, universal tints, artist's oil paints, or japan colors with a transparent alkyd glazing medium and mineral spirits. Many decorative painters prefer to use custom-mixed alkyd paint—the color selected from the manufacturer's color-chip system—because these colors are consistent, easily and accurately reproduced, and fairly inexpensive. Using them also saves time and effort. However, you can also mix your own by coloring white alkyd paint with universal tints, artist's oil paints, or japan colors.

Measure out and pour a small quantity of glazing medium into a small container. Add the colorant drop by drop and stir with a mixing stick until it's thoroughly diffused throughout the medium. Make the color slightly darker than the final hue you want because the mineral spirits will lighten it.

When you have the exact color that you want, mix in the mineral spirits until you achieve the desired consistency. Test the result on your sample board, allow it to dry, and make any necessary adjustments to the color. As always, cover the glaze and note the formula in your record book.

If you want to do things the old-fashioned way and mix your own glazing medium, just combine boiled linseed oil with an equal amount of turpentine or mineral spirits and a few drops of a siccative or dryer (such as terebene dryer or cobalt stannate).

Because of the high percentage of solvent, an oil glaze has a short shelf life, which means you can't store it for more than ten days or so after adding the mineral spirits. If you think you will need to keep a glaze longer than that, blend only the colorant and alkyd glazing medium, cover the mixture tightly, and store. Add the mineral spirits later, just before each time you're ready to use the glaze.

F O R M U L A

BASIC OIL GLAZE

- 1 part custom-mixed alkyd paint, universal tints, artist's oil paints, or japan colors mixed into white alkyd paint

- 1 part alkyd glazing liquid

- 1 part mineral spirits

Some techniques require a looser glaze, called 50-percent glaze. To make it, take this basic oil glaze, and add another one part mineral spirits, which raises the solvent content to 50 percent.

Making and Using an Overglaze

Occasionally, a decorative finish requires an overglaze as a final step. This is a thin glaze, with four times as much thinner as a normal glaze. Either you can use your original glaze thinned somewhat, or you can make a new, thinner glaze in another color, one that softens the existing finish by feathering additional subtle color over its surface.

Because both the glazes are transparent, they will appear to mix into a third color—a pale blue overglaze will make a yellow glaze underneath it look slightly green.

F O R M U L A

BASIC OVERGLAZE

- 1 part custom-mixed colored latex or alkyd paint, or white latex or alkyd paint colored with the appropriate colorant

- 1 part latex or alkyd glazing medium, as appropriate

- 4 parts thinner, as appropriate

An overglaze *can soften the look of a finish, much as a layer of gauze would. A soft green can be produced by applying a pale blue overglaze over a yellow glaze.*

Applying the Glaze

There are two ways to apply a glaze over a painted base coat:

- The positive technique involves adding the glaze to the surface using random or scattered strokes with a tool such as a sponge, rolled rag, or brush
- The negative technique involves applying the glaze to the entire surface and then removing some of it with a tool such as a sponge or graining comb

With the positive technique, the easier method of the two, the glaze goes directly over the base coat. It may be necessary to apply several layers of glaze this way. Each layer must dry before you add the next one, but this isn't a problem. There is no need to hurry, and one person working alone can accomplish this technique with relative ease.

Sponging on *a glaze with random strokes makes these walls look texturous.*

The negative technique is significantly more challenging because the glaze must be applied over the painted base coat and then removed. This means you can work with the glaze only while it's still wet.

This wet stage is short in duration—and the drier and hotter your local weather conditions, the faster the drying time will be. You have only about 10 to 25 minutes of wet, or open, time with alkyd glazes, and only 8 to 15 minutes with faster-drying latex glazes. (Adding a gel retardant will slow a latex glaze's drying time—helpful if you're a beginner or working alone.) During this time you can do anything you want to the glaze, including reworking it, adding to it, smoothing it out, and repairing it. Once the wet time elapses, you have reached *snap time*, which means the glaze has become slightly tacky. From then on anything you do to the glaze—for example, any of the negative techniques—will damage it. However, you do have time to remove it and start over, if you wish.

Snap time is reached within 20 to 35 minutes for alkyd glazes, 10 to 20 minutes for latex. At that point the glaze will feel dry to the touch, and you may still be able to remove it with some difficulty. To avoid problems, it's best not to dawdle.

Complicated negative techniques, especially on large surfaces, require two people working as a team to do the job right. One person applies the glaze in strips 2 to 3 feet wide, while the second person follows, working the negative technique. Both must work quickly. Experiment with the technique beforehand so you can determine how large a section you can handle at one time and to develop a rhythm for working in tandem.

When you're glazing all the walls in a room, it's best to glaze opposite walls first, letting them dry completely, before applying the glaze to the remaining walls.

The amount of glaze you remove will determine how much of the base-coat color will show through. Leaving lots of glaze on the surface creates an opaque, or closed, texture that will hide much of the base coat. Conversely, removing lots of glaze creates an open, translucent texture that will allow much of the base coat to be visible. You can also get an open look by using less glaze, making numerous passes with the removal tool, or using heavy pressure on the tool in a single pass.

Many things affect the success of your glazing project. (See "Common Glaze Problems" on page 124.) The following are especially important for getting good results:

- Maintain the consistency of your glaze. Its thinner, especially mineral spirits, can evaporate while you're working
- Use clean tools that are in good condition so you can remove glaze evenly. Once a tool becomes loaded with glaze, it doesn't perform properly. Either clean it or replace it
- Exert uniform pressure and make consistent strokes with tools so that the glazed surface displays an even finish

SOLVING COMMON GLAZE PROBLEMS

PROBLEM	CAUSE	CURE
1. Glaze sags on a vertical surface	A. Glaze too thin B. Base too shiny	Remove glaze, thicken, and reapply
2. Glaze sags on a horizontal surface	Same as 1	Same as 1
3. Glaze is too dry	A. Too little applied B. Too much removed	Remove glaze and reapply
4. Holes appear in glaze	Uneven tool pressure	Rework wet glaze; feather in new glaze if old glaze is dry
5. Corners and edges blotchy	Same as 4	Same as 4
6. Corners and edges too light	Same as 4	Same as 4
7. Dark spots in glazed surface	A. Uneven tool pressure B. Too much glaze C. Too little glaze D. Dirty tool	A. Darken area around spots B. Overglaze C. Feather in more glaze D. Clean tool frequently
8. Surface flaws highlighted by glaze	Unsealed or improperly primed surface	A. Overglaze B. Let glaze dry; feather darker glaze around imperfections
9. Glaze gradually becomes darker and less transparent	A. Solvent has evaporated B. Too little glaze removed	A. If wet, thin glaze to right thickness, dry, remove glaze, and reapply B. If dry, remove glaze with solvent and reapply
10. Glaze is too dry or won't keep wet edge	A. Solvent has evaporated B. Working too large an area at one time C. Improper (flat latex) base painting	A. Balance glaze/solvent ratio B. Add retardant to slow drying time, or coat surface with solvent to extend working time C. Work a smaller area
11. Wet edge is darker when dry	Applied glaze over wet edge, not up to it	A. If wet, remove and reapply B. If dry, overglaze C. Add glaze around lines in random pattern to disguise them

PART II

The Decorative Painting Techniques

Sponging is a good place to start the exploration of the specific decorative painting techniques and all of their variations. Starting with sponging also seems appropriate because it is the easiest and most versatile decorative paint finish. Realistically, it's also one of the most tedious, especially if you're decorating large areas such as all of the walls in a room. Your hand will touch every inch of those walls many times over before the job is done. Keep this in mind when you're considering any finish.

Sponging

This doesn't negate the beauty of the technique. Sponging creates a dappled finish, a subtle play of color that ranges from delicate to bold. Certainly, the dazzling result is worth the effort. It all depends on the colors you choose, the transparency and glossiness of your glaze, and how heavily you apply it.

Subtle tonal variations *create a sophisticated effect on walls with sponged-on color.*

Starting with simple sponging helps you learn a number of important skills, including mixing paint and glaze, applying a glaze properly, getting a feeling for the decorative paint process, and developing coordination of your eye and hand.

Because it produces a textured surface with great visual depth, sponging disguises imperfect walls and hides dirt in hard-use areas such as children's rooms. It's also a way to enhance furniture made of inexpensive wood.

Appropriately, the technique takes its name from the only tool usually used to apply the finish, a sponge. Not just any sponge, however. It must be a natural sea sponge, the only sponge that has the irregular shape and uneven surface necessary to create a mottled texture. Sea sponges come in round and flat shapes and are sold in paint and craft stores. The flat shape works best for sponging (always use the flat side, which was attached to the rock). If you can't find a flat sponge, cut a round sea sponge in half to create a similar effect. If you use the sponge correctly, you won't be able to see the individual strokes of paint on the wall.

Apply the glaze quickly; you could use a fast-drying latex or acrylic glaze in most cases. If you use a water-based glaze, immediately correct any mistakes you make with a clean sponge and water. Slower-drying oil glazes also work well with this technique. Whatever type of glaze you use, you'll need a damp sponge. Prepare it by dipping it into clean water and wringing it out until the sponge is damp but not wet.

A natural sea sponge
has the uneven, irregular texture required for creating a mottled finish.

As with most decorative finishes, individual strokes shouldn't be visible when they're done. To achieve this subtle effect, apply the glaze over a color-coordinated base coat that is thoroughly dry.

To make the proper stroke, hold the sponge flat and, working from your wrist, quickly and lightly pounce it straight up and down over the surface of the wall. Don't let the sponge slip or slide on the glaze. Apply each stroke of the sponge so that it just barely touches the last one, and work consistently across the surface—don't hop around the room sponging at random or the effect will be uneven. Give the sponge a one-quarter turn before you make each stroke, and turn your hand from side to side to avoid any tendency to create an identifiable pattern. To sponge into corners, cut off a small piece of the sponge to make a flat edge.

About 40 percent of the base-coat color will show through when you finish the first sponged coat. The second sponged coat will overlap some of the base color and some of the first sponged strokes, covering about 40 percent of the wall. When you're finished, about 25 percent of the base-coat color will be visible.

Effective sponging keeps color contrasts to a minimum and puts the emphasis on subtle tonal variations of a single hue or several closely related hues of glaze applied over a pale or light base. As you become more secure with the technique, try for more dramatic color combinations. Several striking variations are mentioned with the techniques presented in the chapter.

Sponging

- Sponging On: Two Colors

- Sponging On: Three Colors

- Random Sponging: Four Colors

- Sponging Off: One Color

Sponging On: Two Colors

This is the basic sponging technique. It is a positive, or additive, method, which means you dab glaze over the base coat (as opposed to sponging it off) to create the desired effect.

First, the surface receives a light base coat. When it's thoroughly dry, sponge on two slightly contrasting coats of glaze using the application method described on the previous page. Let the first coat dry before applying the second coat.

In the examples, the base coat is a warm white paint applied with a roller. The first sponged coat is a medium taupe; the second sponged coat, a deep golden beige. Custom-mixed latex paints were used as the colorants and then blended with an acrylic glazing medium and water to make a slightly opaque, fast-drying finish. Use artist's acrylics for the colorant if you want a more translucent finish. You might want to add a gel retarder to the glaze beforehand to slow down drying and allow more time to work.

How to Sponge on Two Colors

1   Mix the first glaze to the desired color and thickness. Pour a small amount into the paint tray. Hold a dampened sponge flat side down, and dip it into the glaze. Gently slide the sponge over the ridges so that it becomes evenly coated with glaze. Off-load any excess glaze onto old newspapers so that your first stroke isn't filled with too much glaze.

2   Sponge the surface as described in the introduction, pages 128–129. Avoid creating an identifiable pattern. Reload and off-load the sponge with glaze as often as necessary. This first step covers about 40 percent of the base coat. Let the glaze dry.

3 Repeat Step 2 with the second color, sponging it on so that it covers about 40 percent of the wall. Let it dry.

4 The final finish reveals about 25 percent of the base-coat color. The overlapping light and dark areas create the illusion of depth and texture. Also note how the individual sponge strokes are indistinguishable from one another.

A VARIATION: Use this method to apply two coats of light glaze over a dark base coat. The result adds dramatic flair to a room. Be sure to constantly vary your strokes because a repetitive pattern is more noticeable when you put light glazes over a dark base coat.

F O R M U L A

SPONGING ON: TWO COLORS (Positive Method 1)

SKILL LEVEL: Beginner

RECOMMENDED FOR: Any flat or smooth surface, including floors and ceilings. Especially good for walls with flaws that need hiding and in hard-use areas such as children's rooms. Also good for furniture that doesn't have intricate carving or elaborate trim

NOT RECOMMENDED FOR: Uneven surfaces with intricate carving or elaborate trim

PAIRS OF HANDS NEEDED: 1

TOOLS: Paint buckets; mixing sticks; paint tray; sea sponges; bucket of clear water; old newspaper; clean rags; gloves

BASE COAT: Latex paint

GLAZE COLORANTS: Custom-mixed eggshell latex paints or artist's acrylics, or custom-mixed eggshell alkyd paints or universal tints

GLAZE FORMULA: For a latex glaze— 1 part colorant, 1 part latex or acrylic glazing medium, and 1 part water. For an oil glaze—1 part colorant, 1 part alkyd glazing medium, and 1 part mineral spirits

TYPICAL WORKABLE SECTION: A 2-foot-wide wall or surface

CLEAR TOP COAT: Optional

Sponging On: Three Colors

This technique results in a denser surface than the first sponging-on method, so less of the base coat will show through. Use three glazes over a light base coat to create the finish. In this example, the glaze colors are the taupe and golden beige used in the first method, with a dark terra-cotta color accent. They are slightly opaque and fast-drying glazes made with equal parts of custom-mixed latex paint, acrylic glazing medium, and water. For a more translucent look, use artist's acrylics for the latex paint.

COVERING PERCENTAGES

Why don't the coverage percentages equal 100? Here's how these numbers work: when you cover 40 percent of the base coat, 60 percent of it still shows through. When a second coat covers 40 percent of the whole wall, it covers 40 percent of both the first coat and the base coat. Of the 60 percent of the base coat that was showing after the first coat, just 60 percent of *that* is now showing, or about 25 percent (0.6 x 0.6 = 0.24). A third coat covering 40 percent of the wall will allow 60 percent of this fraction to show: 0.24 x 0.6 = 0.96, or about 10 percent.

How to Sponge on Three Colors

1   *Mix the first glaze to the desired color and thickness. Pour a small amount into the paint tray. Reseal the can to prevent spills. Hold the dampened sponge flat side down, and dip it into the glaze. Gently slide it over the ridges so it becomes evenly coated with glaze. Off-load any excess glaze onto old newspapers. You don't want your first stroke filled with too much glaze.*

2   *Sponge the surface following the instruction in the introduction, pages 128–129. Avoid creating an identifiable pattern. Reload and off-load the sponge with glaze as often as necessary to create a consistent look. This step covers about 40 percent of the base coat. Let the glaze dry.*

3 Repeat Step 2 with the second color, sponging it on so that it covers about 40 percent of the wall. Let it dry. Apply the third color using the same technique. It should cover about 40 percent of the wall. Let it dry.

4 The final finish reveals about 10 percent of the base-coat color. The overlapping light and dark areas create the illusion of depth and texture. Also note how the individual sponge strokes are indistinguishable from one another.

F O R M U L A

SPONGING ON: THREE COLORS
(Positive Method 2)

SKILL LEVEL: Beginner

SKILL LEVEL: Beginner to intermediate

RECOMMENDED FOR: Any flat or smooth surface, including floors and ceilings. Especially good for walls with flaws that need hiding and for hard-use areas such as children's rooms. Also works well on furniture that does not have intricate trim

NOT RECOMMENDED FOR: Surfaces with intricate carving or elaborate trim

PAIRS OF HANDS NEEDED: 1

TOOLS: Paint buckets; mixing sticks; paint tray; sea sponge; bucket of water for cleaning sponge; newspapers; clean rags; gloves

BASE COAT: Latex paint

GLAZE COLORANTS: Custom-mixed eggshell latex paints or artist's acrylics, or alkyd paints or universal tints

GLAZE FORMULA: For a latex glaze— 1 part colorant, 1 part acrylic or latex glazing medium, and 1 part water. For an oil glaze—1 part colorant, 1 part alkyd glazing medium, and 1 part mineral spirits

TYPICAL WORKABLE SECTION: A 2-foot-wide wall or surface

CLEAR TOP COAT: Optional

Random Sponging: Four Colors

This method involves a slightly different sponging technique. It's called *random* because of the loose arrangement of the strokes. The effect is a texture that is more ephemeral or diffused and very close to color washing in some respects. It gets away from the tight texture of the first two sponging-on techniques by letting you drag the sponge lightly to roughen the surface and blend the colors as you make your strokes. Random sponging creates a colorful, painterly look that's particularly appropriate for doors, small walls such as accent or transition walls, and unornamented furniture.

In this example, the finish is accomplished by applying four colors of glaze—golden beige, green, taupe, and warm white— over a warm-white base coat. The warm-white glaze acts as an overglaze, softening and blending the overall color but still allowing the individual hues to peek through.

Remember to let the base coat thoroughly dry before applying the finish colors.

How to Random Sponge Four Colors

1 *Mix the first glaze, prepare the sponge, and sponge on the glaze as described in the first two steps of "Sponging On: Two Colors," page 130. However, as your sponge touches the surface in the straight up and down pouncing motion, shift it slightly to get the blending effect shown. Keep the strokes more random than those in sponging on, covering only 30 percent of the base coat. Let the glaze dry.*

2 *Mix the second color, and apply it the same way. Use a random pattern that allows areas of the first glaze to remain untouched. Let the glaze dry.*

3 *Mix the third color, and apply it to the surface, filling in areas left untouched by the second glaze. Let the glaze dry.*

4 *The thinned-out fourth color is almost transparent. Pat it over the entire surface using a light touch, overlapping and filling in areas as needed.*

F O R M U L A

RANDOM SPONGING: FOUR COLORS
(Positive Method 3)

SKILL LEVEL: Advanced beginner to intermediate

RECOMMENDED FOR: Small walls, doors, and other flat surfaces free of intricate carving or elaborate trim, as well as furniture with little or no ornamentation

NOT RECOMMENDED FOR: Ceilings or areas with intricate carving or elaborate trim or ornate furniture

PAIRS OF HANDS NEEDED: 1

TOOLS: Paint buckets; mixing sticks; paint tray; 4 sea sponges; bucket of clear water; mineral spirits; old newspapers; clean rags; gloves

BASE COAT: Latex paint

GLAZE COLORANTS: Custom-mixed latex paints or artist's acrylics, or custom-mixed alkyd paints or universal tints

GLAZE FORMULA: For a latex glaze—1 part colorant, 1 part acrylic or latex glazing medium, and 1 part water. For an oil glaze—1 part colorant, 1 part alkyd glazing medium, and 1 part mineral spirits

TYPICAL WORKABLE SECTION: A 2-foot-wide wall or surface

CLEAR TOP COAT: Optional

Sponging Off: One Color

This is a negative, or subtractive, method of sponging, which means putting on the glaze with a sponge and then lifting some of it off with another sponge. Like random sponging, it produces a subtly blended finish, less structured than that created by the standard sponging-on methods.

This method requires two people, one to apply the glaze and one to take it off. The glazer shouldn't get too far ahead of the sponger, or the paint will reach snap time too early, which means starting over. On the other hand, you mustn't remove the glaze immediately, or what remains on the surface will run. Experiment with the technique to gauge the timing and the area you have to cover so that you can be comfortable working it. Remember, the glazing partner can work much faster than the one working the sponge.

In this example, a medium rose-beige oil glaze made with custom-mixed alkyd paint, alkyd glazing medium, and solvent is applied over a base coat of warm-white latex paint. If desired, use universal tints as the colorant. Do not use a latex or acrylic glaze for this technique, as it does not give you sufficient working time.

How to Sponge Off One Color

1 Mix the glaze to the desired color and thickness. Pour a small amount into a paint tray. Reseal the can to keep the solvent from evaporating. Prepare the damp sponge, and then sponge the glaze onto the surface using the technique described in the introduction, pages 128–129. Make sure each stroke touches and occasionally overlaps the previous stroke. Let about 20 percent of the base-coat color show through.

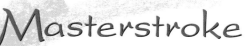

Masterstroke

After working the technique on a small surface, you can expedite the drying time of the oil-based glaze by using a blow dryer or by adding a dryer (such as terebene dryer, copal medium, or light-drying oil) to the glaze formula.

2 *Using a clean, damp sponge, lift off as much of the glaze as possible. As you go along, the sponge will dry, causing glaze to build up on it. To prevent this, frequently dip the sponge into clean water and wring it out until damp. As you lift off the sponge, occasionally drag it over the glaze (as in Step 1 of "Random Sponging," page 134) to meld the colors together.*

3 *The final finish. About 10 percent of the base color shows through, and the entire surface has a delicate, misty appearance.*

F O R M U L A

SPONGING OFF: ONE COLOR (Negative Method 1)

SKILL LEVEL: Advanced beginner to intermediate

RECOMMENDED FOR: Any flat surface that is free of intricate carving or elaborate trim

NOT RECOMMENDED FOR: Ceilings, flat surface with intricate carving or trim, and small pieces of furniture

PAIRS OF HANDS NEEDED: 2

TOOLS: Paint bucket; mixing sticks; paint tray; two sea sponges; several buckets of clean water; old newspapers; clean rags; mineral spirits; gloves

BASE COAT: Latex paint

GLAZE COLORANT: Custom-mixed eggshell or satin alkyd paint or universal tints

GLAZE FORMULA: 1 part colorant, 1 part alkyd glazing medium, and 1 part mineral spirits

TYPICAL WORKABLE SECTION: A 2-foot-wide wall or surface

CLEAR TOP COAT: Optional

Sponging Off:
One Color, alternative

This negative method uses a paintbrush or roller, a sponge, and cheesecloth to produce another delicate, misty texture that is very pleasing. Similar to "Sponging Off One Color" on the previous page, this technique requires two workers—one to apply the glaze and another to remove it. Although timing is crucial, the technique is not nearly as difficult to work because multiple stroking levels the glaze, making it possible for the glazer to begin removing it immediately. Experiment with both timing and technique before you begin, so you can develop a rhythm for working.

In this example, a reddish-taupe oil glaze is worked over a base coat of warm-white latex paint. The paint was allowed to dry thoroughly before the glaze was applied with a roller.

The real trick is mixing the glaze to the right consistency. The glaze must be thin enough to cover the surface easily, but not too thin or it won't adhere to it. It's a good idea to test a few samples on a practice board before starting your project. Another tip: It's better to remove too much glaze rather than too little. You can always go over the surface with more glaze.

How to Sponge Off One Color

1 Mix a wet, almost runny glaze to the desired color. Pour a small amount into a paint tray.

2 Using a brush or roller, apply the glaze with three sets of crisscross strokes—first, vertical strokes top to bottom; second, horizontal strokes side to side; and third, vertical strokes top to bottom. This sets up the glaze for sponging off.

Masterstroke

For a more mottled or variegated finished effect, vary the way that you move the sponge to remove the glaze. Alternate between dabbing, rolling, and dragging it around in the wet glaze, but always rinse it and wring it out when paint begins to build up in it.

3 Lightly pounce a damp sponge over the wet glaze to remove some of it. Turn the sponge to avoid creating an identifiable pattern. Each stroke should just touch the previous one so about half the glaze is lifted off. Rinse the sponge, and wring it until damp as often as necessary to prevent glaze buildup.

4 Use a dampened fresh sponge to work over the glaze, patting it with the sponge as you make a twisting motion with your hand. This will soften and blend the strokes together. Clean the sponge often to prevent glaze buildup.

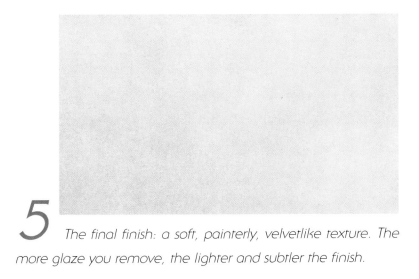

5 The final finish: a soft, painterly, velvetlike texture. The more glaze you remove, the lighter and subtler the finish.

FORMULA

**SPONGING OFF:
ONE COLOR
(Negative Method 2)**

SKILL LEVEL: Advanced beginner to intermediate

RECOMMENDED FOR: Any flat surface, including floors, that is free of intricate carving or elaborate trim, as well as furniture free of intricate ornamentation

NOT RECOMMENDED FOR: Ceilings or any other surface with intricate carving or elaborate trim

PAIRS OF HANDS NEEDED: 2

TOOLS: Paint buckets; mixing sticks; paint tray; 200-grit sandpaper; sea sponges; 90-weight cheesecloth; clean water; clean rags; mineral spirits; gloves

BASE COAT: Latex paint

GLAZE COLORANT: Custom-mixed eggshell or semigloss alkyd, or universal tints

GLAZE FORMULA: 1 part colorant, 1 part alkyd glazing medium, and 1 to 2 parts mineral spirits. Mineral spirits may constitute up to 50 percent of the glaze

TYPICAL WORKABLE SECTION: A 2-foot-wide wall or surface

CLEAR TOP COAT: Optional

More refined than sponging, ragging creates smooth, flowing textures reminiscent of fine materials such as vellum, brushed suede, crushed velvet, and soft leather. Ragging may also go by the names cloth distressing, rag-rolling, and parchment; although they are often used interchangeably, each one refers to a variation on the ragging technique.

Ragging

Ragging techniques are fairly easy to execute. Soft cloth, usually cheesecloth, is either bunched in the hand or rolled and used to apply or lift off wet glaze. Sometimes newspaper is pressed over the glaze to soften and blend the colors before the cloth is worked over the surface. Other materials, such as old sheets and towels, plastic bags, burlap, carpet padding, chamois, and canvas also create an incredible variety of looks. Experiment a little with different ones.

Using a soft, rolled cloth to lift off glaze creates an elegant, smooth texture on a wall.

The finished effect depends on the kind of cloth used and the pressure applied when working it over the glaze, as well as the glossiness and translucence of the glaze. Using newspapers instead of cloth to lift off the glaze will affect it as well. Ragging techniques require two skills not learned with sponging. The first is the ability to bunch or fold the cloth correctly. The second is the knack for working in corners and along edges.

Preparing the Cloth

You'll need 6-foot lengths of cloth. Don't rip them to size; instead, cut them with scissors so you don't have to contend with lint, frayed ends, and loose threads. For ragging on or off, tuck in the cut ends, and bunch up the cloth so that it makes a soft fold in your hand. For rag-rolling off, form the cloth into loose rolls with the ends tucked in. Use the cloth to lift off and blend glaze, executing the stroke described in each technique.

Protecting Adjoining Surfaces

Use painter's masking tape to cover adjoining surfaces such as walls, ceilings, and trim. This tape's microporous edge seals so well that glaze can't seep under it. As you paint each section, dip the flat side of a decorator brush into the glaze, and cut into the corners and borders. Immediately glaze that wall, working back into the corners. Blend the brush strokes with a roller.

Color Choices

Although the most successful ragging techniques use a light-colored glaze over a pale- or light-colored base coat, bright, contrasting colors will yield an equally fine result if carefully worked. All these techniques use a thin oil glaze, so don't neglect your surface preparation. A water-thin glaze seeps into hairline cracks, making them more noticeable.

You must keep a wet edge at all times. It's best to start a new section a little beyond the wet edge and work back into it. This technique keeps the joints between sections from developing an unwanted dark line.

Some of the tools you'll need may include newspaper, a soft cloth, a decorator brush, a roller, and painter's masking tape.

Ragging

- Ragging On: One Color
- Ragging On: Two Colors
- Ragging Off: One Color
- Creating a Parchment Effect: One Color
- Creating a Parchment Effect: Two Colors
- Rag-Rolling Off: One Color
- Ragging Off: Cheesecloth Distressing
- Creating a Parchment Effect with Newsprint
- Creating Faux Morocco Leather

Ragging On:
One Color

In one sense, this basic technique might be described as a cloth-distressed version of sponging. It produces a similar mottled look, although the final effect is considerably airier. Even though it appears easy, it isn't. It takes practice to touch the bunched cloth to the surface with just the right amount of pressure so that the cloth makes a mark without losing its shape or falling out of your hand.

Remember to use a clean cloth that doesn't have any loose or frayed edges, which can leave thread marks on your painted surface. Change cloths often.

Don't forget to protect adjoining surfaces, such as a ceiling or trim, with painter's masking tape. Because time is of the essence—you have to work while the glaze is wet—don't worry too much about corners and edges. You can touch up missed spots with an artist's brush later.

In this example, a green glaze is ragged over a warm-white base coat of latex paint that has been allowed to become thoroughly dry. You can use contrasting colors, however, or experiment with contrasting tonal variations as well.

How to Rag on One Color

1   *Mix the glaze to the desired color and thickness. Pour a small amount into the paint tray. Reseal the can to keep the solvent from evaporating.*

2   *Bunch a piece of cheesecloth in your hand, as described in the Masterstroke (opposite). Dip one side of the cloth into the glaze. Gently slide it over the tray's ridges to coat it evenly with glaze. If necessary, off-load excess glaze onto old newspapers; don't fill the first strokes with too much glaze.*

3   *Start at the top of the section, and work diagonally down the surface in a random fashion. Gently pounce the bunched cloth straight up and down over the surface, making sure each stroke barely touches the previous one. Don't squeeze the cloth. Before you make each stroke, shift the rag in your hand, and then turn your hand from side to side to avoid creating a recognizable pattern. Keep moving constantly, but don't hop around.*

Reload the cloth with glaze as often as necessary. Step back and check your work frequently to make sure your strokes show even pressure and appear to be random. Use a new piece of cheesecloth with each section.

4 *The final finish. The variation in tone among the strokes is the result of the repeated process of gradually depleting and then reloading the cloth with paint as you work. The random tonal gradations add complexity to the look.*

Masterstroke

Much of the success of this technique is in the way you bunch up the rag. Don't create a tight wad of cloth in your hand. Let it form a relaxed ball, which will render a much more natural effect. Practice before applying the first stroke.

FORMULA

RAGGING ON:
ONE COLOR
(Positive Method 1)

SKILL LEVEL: Beginner

RECOMMENDED FOR: Large, flat surfaces such as walls

NOT RECOMMENDED FOR: Ceilings, floors, or any surfaces with intricate carving or elaborate trim

PAIRS OF HANDS NEEDED: 1

TOOLS: Paint buckets; mixing sticks; paint tray; 90-weight cheesecloth; clean rags; mineral spirits; gloves

BASE COAT: Latex paint

GLAZE COLORANT: Custom-mixed alkyd paint or universal tints

GLAZE FORMULA: 1 part colorant, 1 part alkyd glazing medium, and 1 part mineral spirits

TYPICAL WORKABLE SECTION: A 2-foot-wide wall or surface

CLEAR TOP COAT: Optional

Ragging On:
Two Colors

A logical continuation of "Ragging On: One Color," this technique adds a second color glaze to the mix, providing additional depth. You should include this additional step whenever you want a more textural appearance on your surface. If desired, you can extend this method to include a third color glaze. Allow alkyd glaze to dry overnight before applying another color on top of it. Latex formulas dry much faster. (See the box "Average Drying Times," on page 61.)

Whenever you have two or more glaze coats of different values, always apply the lightest glaze first and the darkest glaze .last. You should work dark into light for a practical reason: Dark glazes hold their color better than light glazes. That means light glazes have difficulty holding their own when worked into a darker glaze, so for the best result, follow this advice.

In this example, the base coat is a warm-white latex paint. The first glaze coat is a warm beige; the second glaze coat, the same green color used in first method, which is described on page 144.

How to Rag on Two Colors

1 *Prepare numerous soft sheets of cheesecloth as instructed in the introduction (page 142). Follow Steps 1, 2, and 3 in "Ragging On: One Color," page 144, to mix and apply the lightest-color glaze. Let it dry. Add the second color or darker glaze, starting at the top and working diagonally down the surface.*

2 *The final effect is a randomly textured, more intense finish than that created by one color. Note that you can't see the individual strokes when the surface is done.*

F O R M U L A

RAGGING ON:
TWO COLORS
(Positive Method 2)

SKILL LEVEL: Advanced beginner to intermediate

RECOMMENDED FOR: All large, flat surfaces, especially walls and trim

NOT RECOMMENDED FOR: Ceilings or floors

PAIRS OF HANDS NEEDED: 1

TOOLS: Paint buckets; mixing sticks; paint tray; 6-foot-long pieces of cheesecloth; clean rags; mineral spirits; gloves

BASE COAT: Latex paint

GLAZE COLORANTS: Custom-mixed alkyd paint or universal tints

GLAZE FORMULA: 1 part colorant, 1 part alkyd glazing medium, and 1 part solvent

TYPICAL WORKABLE SECTION: A 2-foot-wide wall or surface

CLEAR TOP COAT: Optional

This painted-on texture *wakes up plain walls and adds drama to an ordinary space.*

Ragging Off:
One Color

Sometimes referred to as cheeseclothing, this negative glazing method requires two people: one to roll on the glaze and another to lift it off, while it is still wet, with large bunched-up pieces of cloth. Timing is critical with most negative techniques because the glaze can be rolled on more quickly than it can be lifted off. Experiment beforehand to determine how large a section you and your partner can work on at one time, taking skill into consideration. An oil-based glaze will allow you more time to work than a latex-based formula because it takes longer to dry. (See the box "Average Drying Times" on page 61.) Keep this in mind when planning your project.

Remember to use a clean cloth that doesn't have any frayed edges. You don't want deposits of little strands of thread to mar your finish.

In this example, a taupe oil glaze is worked over a base coat of warm-white latex paint that is thoroughly dry.

How to Rag Off One Color

1 *Prepare the cheesecloth as instructed in the introduction (page 142). Mix the glaze to the desired color and thickness, and pour a little into the paint tray. Reseal the can to keep the solvent from evaporating.*

2 *Using a roller or paintbrush, lay the glaze over the entire section in three sets of crisscross strokes—first, vertical strokes, moving from top to bottom; second, horizontal strokes, moving side to side; and third, vertical strokes, from top to bottom once more. This multiple stroking sets up the glaze and levels it.*

3 *Working from the wrist, your partner should lightly pounce a bunched cloth over the wet surface, picking up the glaze. Continually shift the cloth so new folds are exposed with each stroke. Turn the hand from side to side so a recognizable pattern does not take shape. When the cloth starts putting glaze back onto the surface, change to a clean cloth. Repeat.*

4 *The final finish has a lush texture that resembles suede. The illusion is so realistic and appealing that you may be tempted to touch it. Note that lines between sections don't show. You can't find the individual strokes either.*

Masterstroke

After you've finished, stand back and take a good look at the surface for any breaks or obvious patterning. While the glaze is still wet, you can go over a section that may be too dense with glaze, using a clean cloth. If necessary, fill in areas that are too light with a little more color.

FORMULA

**RAGGING OFF:
ONE COLOR
(Negative Method 1)**

SKILL LEVEL: Advanced beginner to intermediate

RECOMMENDED FOR: Large, flat surfaces, especially walls, and trim

NOT RECOMMENDED FOR: Ceilings or floors. Also a waste of time for very small surfaces

PAIRS OF HANDS NEEDED: 2

TOOLS: Paint buckets; mixing sticks; paint tray; roller with a ¼-inch nap or foam cover or paintbrush properly sized to the surface; artist's brushes for touching up; 90-weight cheesecloth cut into 6-foot-long pieces; clean rags; mineral spirits; gloves

BASE COAT: Latex paint

GLAZE COLORANT: Custom-mixed alkyd paint or universal tints

GLAZE FORMULA: 1 part colorant, 1 part alkyd glazing medium, and 1 part mineral spirits

TYPICAL WORKABLE SECTION: A 2-foot-wide wall or surface

CLEAR TOP COAT: Optional

Creating a Parchment Effect: One Color

Think of parchment, the kind medieval monks used, and you'll understand this technique's appeal. It makes a sumptuous wash of luminous color and soft texture. Happily, it's as easy to do as it is attractive. However, as with all negative techniques, you'll need two people to execute it: one to apply the glaze and one to blend it.

Once your base coat is dry, your only concerns are mixing the glaze, applying one coat, and pulling some of it off with a cloth. You don't even have to work carefully, except in the corners of walls.

In this example, the parchment method is worked with a medium beige glaze over a base coat of warm-white latex paint. Brush or roll on the base coat in the traditional way, depending on the size of the surface. Once the paint is thoroughly dry, lay on the oil glaze. Always use a clean cloth that doesn't have frayed edges. Deposits of small threads can mar your finish.

How to Create a One-Color Parchment Finish

1 *Mix the glaze to the desired color and thickness, and pour a small amount into the paint tray. Reseal the can to keep the solvent from evaporating.*

2 *Dip the roller or brush into the glaze mixture, and run it over the tray's ridges to evenly coat it. Off-load excess glaze onto old newspapers; don't fill the first strokes with too much glaze.*

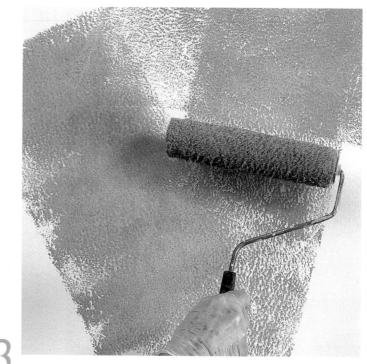

3 *Cut in the glaze along all the borders in the first section. Working from top to bottom, apply the glaze onto the wall, making loose, M-shaped strokes with the roller, as shown. (See "Base Coating," pages 101–103.) Leave about 20 percent of the base coat showing. Work quickly so that you keep a wet edge.*

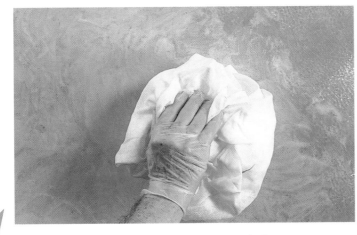

4 Holding a piece of bunched cheesecloth, your partner should swirl the wet glaze around to blend it. Then take a clean piece of cheesecloth, bunch it up in the same way, and—using a light, quick, straight up-and-down pouncing stroke—texture the glaze. When the area is dry, mix the overglaze. Bunch up more cheesecloth, and pat the new glaze over the entire surface. Let the surface dry. This step calms down the look and puts a soft finish over the entire surface.

5 The final finish. A hint: As you apply glaze to a new section, start a few inches in from the wet edge, and work back into it to mask the meeting line.

F O R M U L A

CREATING A PARCHMENT EFFECT: ONE COLOR
(Negative Method 2)

SKILL LEVEL: Advanced beginner to intermediate

RECOMMENDED FOR: Large, flat surfaces, especially walls

NOT RECOMMENDED FOR: Ceilings, floors, or any surface with intricate carving or elaborate trim

PAIRS OF HANDS NEEDED: 2

TOOLS: Painter's masking tape; paint buckets; mixing sticks; paint tray; roller with a ¼-inch nap or foam cover or paintbrush properly sized to the surface; artist's brushes for touching up; 90-weight cheesecloth cut into 6-foot-long pieces; clean rags; mineral spirits; gloves

BASE COAT: Latex paint

GLAZE COLORANT: Custom-mixed alkyd paint or universal tints

GLAZE FORMULA: 1 part colorant, 1 part alkyd glazing medium, and 1 part solvent

OVERGLAZE: 1 part colorant, 1 part alkyd glazing medium and 4 parts mineral spirits

TYPICAL WORKABLE SECTION: A 2-foot-wide wall or surface

CLEAR TOP COAT: Optional

Creating a Parchment Effect: Two Colors

This parchment method is the same as that described in "Creating a Parchment Effect: One Color," pages 150–151, except that you'll roll on a second glaze color as an accent. It gives you more color (although subtly) and a greater sense of depth.

Don't forget to protect adjacent areas, such as the ceiling or trim, with painter's masking tape.

If you skip a spot or make a mistake, simply let the glaze dry, and then go back the next day to fix it. For skipped areas, especially in corners or around trim, use a brush to feather in some full-strength glaze. If some areas are too light, thin the glaze, and feather it over the existing coat using an artist's brush. This will heighten the color. If you think some areas are too dark, make a lighter version of the glaze, and feather it over those places using an artist's brush.

Always work with a clean rag that doesn't have frayed edges. Deposits of small threads can mar your finish.

How to Create a Two-Color Parchment Finish

1 Follow steps 1–3, "Creating a Parchment Effect: One Color," page 150, to get started. Immediately after you've rolled on the first glaze color, roll on the second, darker glaze so that you cover about 50 percent of the surface. Let about 20 percent of your base coat show through.

2 Swirl the glazes together, and then texture and over-glaze the surface as described in steps 4 and 5, "Creating a Parchment Effect: One Color," page 151.

3 The final finish: Although similar to "Creating a Parchment Effect: One Color," it has greater depth, texture, and luminosity.

Masterstroke

As a variation, you may want to create a fresco effect. To do this, apply the first color. When it dries, lightly sand over it. Wipe off or vacuum away dust particles; then apply the second color over the shaded surface. While the second glaze is still wet, rub the color vigorously into the surface. When it's thoroughly dry, the effect should be lustrous. Experiment with this method on a sample board.

FORMULA

CREATING A PARCHMENT EFFECT: TWO COLORS (Negative Method 3)

SKILL LEVEL: Advanced beginner to intermediate

RECOMMENDED FOR: Large, flat surfaces, especially walls

NOT RECOMMENDED FOR: Ceilings, floors, or any surface with intricate carving or elaborate trim

PAIRS OF HANDS NEEDED: 2

TOOLS: Painter's masking tape; paint buckets; mixing sticks; 2 paint trays; 2 rollers with ¼-inch nap or foam covers or 2 decorator brushes properly sized to the surface; artist's brushes for touching up; cheesecloth cut into 6-foot-long pieces; clean rags; mineral spirits; gloves

BASE COAT: Latex paint

GLAZE COLORANTS: Custom-mixed alkyd paints or universal tints

GLAZE FORMULA: 1 part colorant, 1 part alkyd glazing medium, and 1 part mineral spirits

OVERGLAZE FORMULA: 1 part colorant, 1 part alkyd glazing medium, and 2 to 3 parts mineral spirits

TYPICAL WORKABLE SECTION: A 2-foot-wide wall or surface

CLEAR TOP COAT: Optional

Rag-Rolling Off: One Color

As strange as it may seem, the look of crumpled parchment makes a handsome surface, one rich with striking variations in texture and color. A moderately easy method to execute, it involves rolling a rag through wet glaze and lifting it off in a rhythmic pattern. Because this is a negative method, it requires two people—one to roll on the glaze and one to roll it off. The hardest part of the technique is moving the rag down the wall with an even, steady stroke. Practice first: Not only will this hone your skill, but it will teach you how much area the glazer can cover without getting too far ahead of the rag roller. This method works best on a large surface with a light base coat and a slightly darker glaze coat.

In this example, a beige oil glaze goes over a base coat of warm-white latex paint. The glaze is thinner than the standard oil glaze, and it's not applied until the base coat is thoroughly cured.

Don't forget to keep extra clean rags on hand, and never use ones with frayed edges. Deposits of small threads can mar your finish.

How to Rag-Roll Off

1 Prepare old sheeting or another soft fabric as described in the introduction (page 142), or use 90-weight cheesecloth that's been laundered several times to soften it. Form the pieces into loose rolls with the ends tucked in.

2 Mix the glaze to the desired color and thickness, and pour a small amount into a tray. Roll it evenly over the base coat using three sets of crisscross strokes—first, vertical strokes, top to bottom; second, horizontal strokes; third, vertical strokes. This sets up the glaze; don't let it build up, or it will get too thick and too dark.

3 Your partner should then roll a prepared cloth through the glaze, working from top to bottom. Shift the cloth around to *limit saturation and to avoid a repetitive pattern. When the cloth starts putting glaze back on the wall, get a fresh one. Overlap sections slightly to avoid producing a definite line. Keep checking for any recognizable pattern. If one develops, pat it out, feather in additional glaze, and roll off again.*

4 Go over the glazed surface a second time with fresh rolls of cloth. This further softens and blends the pattern.

5 The final finish. The treated surface displays an even, richly textural appearance.

F O R M U L A

RAG-ROLLING OFF: ONE COLOR (Negative Method 4)

SKILL LEVEL: Intermediate

RECOMMENDED FOR: Large, flat surfaces, especially walls

NOT RECOMMENDED FOR: Ceiling, floors, or any surface with intricate carving or elaborate trim

PAIRS OF HANDS NEEDED: 2

TOOLS: Painter's masking tape; paint bucket; mixing sticks; paint tray; a roller with a ¼-inch nap or foam cover or a decorator brush properly sized to the surface; 90-weight cheesecloth or other soft fabric cut into 6-foot-long pieces; artist's brush for touching up; clean rags; mineral spirits; gloves

BASE COAT: Latex paint

GLAZE COLORANT: Custom-mixed alkyd paint or universal tints

GLAZE FORMULA: 1 part colorant, 1 part alkyd glazing medium, and 2 parts mineral spirits

TYPICAL WORKABLE SECTION: A 2-foot-wide wall or surface

CLEAR TOP COAT: Optional

Ragging Off: Cheesecloth Distressing

Here's another elegant variation. It starts with ragging off, which provides more contrast, and ends with cheesecloth distressing to create a soft, blended look. A negative method, it requires two workers—one to lay on the glaze and one to lift it off. Before you start, practice to gauge the size of the area the two of you can work comfortably, master the technique, and develop a working rhythm.

Don't forget to protect adjacent areas with painter's masking tape. Also, keep extra clean cloths on hand so that you can change them frequently. Never use cloths that have frayed edges. Deposits of small threads can mar your finish.

As with all the parchment techniques, this requires a thin oil glaze. In this example, one slightly darker glaze coat goes over a thoroughly dry base coat of cool-white latex paint. The one color provides sufficient texture and contrast because it gets worked two ways.

How to Rag Off and Cheesecloth Distress

1   Prepare the cheesecloth as described in the instructions (page 142). Mix the glaze to the desired color and thickness, and pour a small amount into the paint tray. Reseal the can to keep the solvent from evaporating.

2   Lay the glaze over the base coat using a roller or brush. Let as much as 30 percent of the base-coat color show through.

3   With a bunched-up cloth, your partner should quickly pounce it over the glazed surface with straight up-and-down strokes, lifting off glaze using a vigorous stroke. Shift the cloth with each stroke, and turn the hand from side to side. Check the work frequently for patterning. If a pattern develops, pat it out, feather in additional glaze, and pounce the wet area again. When the cloth becomes saturated with glaze, discard it for a new one.

4 When the section has been ragged off, immediately take a clean bunched cloth, and distress the glaze to soften, smooth, and blend it. With each stroke, lightly twist the cloth as it touches the surface to soften the pattern's edges. At this point about 20 percent of the base-coat color still shows through. For a variation on this step, fold the cloth into a flat pad instead of bunching it into loose folds.

5 The final finish. The two-step removal method creates a subtle look that has more texture and depth than that produced by either plain ragging off or cheesecloth distressing alone.

FORMULA

RAGGING OFF: CHEESECLOTH DISTRESSING (Negative Method 5)

SKILL LEVEL: Intermediate

RECOMMENDED FOR: Large, flat surfaces, especially walls

NOT RECOMMENDED FOR: Ceilings, floors, small surfaces, or any surface with intricate carving or elaborate trim

PAIRS OF HANDS NEEDED: 2

TOOLS: Painter's masking tape; paint buckets; mixing sticks; paint tray; a roller cover with a ¼-inch nap or foam cover or a decorator brush properly sized to the surface; 90-weight cheesecloth cut into 6-foot-long pieces; artist's brushes for touching up; clean rags; mineral spirits; gloves

BASE COAT: Latex paint

GLAZE COLORANT: Custom-mixed alkyd paint or universal tints

GLAZE FORMULA: 1 part colorant, 1 part alkyd glaze medium, 2 parts mineral spirits

TYPICAL WORKABLE SECTION: A 2-foot-wide wall or surface

CLEAR TOP COAT: Optional

Creating a Parchment Effect with Newsprint

Although this finish appears similar to the other parchment surfaces, newsprint parchment uses regular newspaper to off-load excess glaze and blend the two glazes. A little of the newspaper's ink soaks into a light-colored glaze, giving it a distinctive accent. There are differences in the inks—and the amounts of ink—used by newspapers. Test out a few before using one to see what effect is produced and whether you like it. If you don't want the subtle ink deposits, use a pad or two of plain newsprint, which you can find at an art-supply store.

As with the negative techniques for traditional parchment, rag-rolling off, and ragging off, this one requires two people to execute it—one to roll on the glaze and the other to blend it while it's still wet. Practice will help you hone your skills and perfect the timing.

Don't forget to protect adjacent areas with painter's masking tape. Also, keep a supply of extra sheets of newspaper and cloths on hand. Never use cloths with frayed edges. Stray strands of thread can mar your finish.

How to Create Newsprint Glaze

1 Follow steps 1–3, "Traditional Parchment: One Color," page 150, to start this finishing treatment. Immediately after you've rolled on the first glaze, roll on the second, darker glaze to cover about 50 percent of the surface.

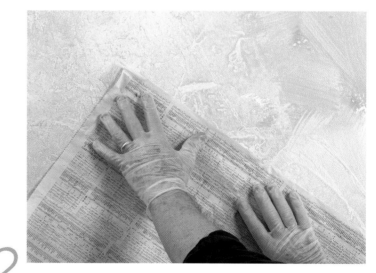

2 Your partner should then open a sheet of newspaper, lay it over the glaze, and press it flat onto the surface. Working at a 45-degree angle, repeat until the entire section has been treated this way. Keep changing the newspaper's angles to avoid creating a recognizable pattern. Note how the ink begins to blend the colors. When a sheet becomes gooey, discard it for a fresh one.

3 Immediately bunch up the cheesecloth as described in the introduction, and swirl the glazes together to soften the straight lines. Then texture, but do not overglaze, as described in steps 4 and 5, "Traditional Parchment: One Color," page 151.

4 The final finish. A subtler version of the two-color traditional parchment technique.

F O R M U L A

CREATING A PARCHMENT EFFECT WITH NEWSPRINT (Negative Method 6)

SKILL LEVEL: Intermediate

RECOMMENDED FOR: Large, flat surfaces, especially walls

NOT RECOMMENDED FOR: Ceilings, floors, or any surface with intricate carving or elaborate trim

PAIRS OF HANDS NEEDED: 2

TOOLS: Painter's masking tape; paint buckets; mixing sticks; two paint trays; two rollers with ¼-inch-nap or foam covers or two decorator brushes properly sized to the surface; artist's brushes for touching up; 90-weight cheesecloth cut into 6-foot-long pieces; newspapers; clean rags; mineral spirits; gloves

BASE COAT: Latex paint

GLAZE COLORANTS: Custom-mixed alkyd paint or universal tints

GLAZE FORMULA: 1 part colorant, 1 part alkyd glazing medium, and 1 part mineral spirits

TYPICAL WORKABLE SECTION: A 2-foot-wide wall or surface

CLEAR TOP COAT: Optional

Creating Faux Morocco Leather

The intrinsic beauty of the ragging techniques reaches full flower with this look. It is intended to imitate morocco, fine leather made from goatskin that has been tanned with sumac. This deep-hued, dramatic faux finish is subtle and sumptuous at the same time. It offers ample evidence that decorative painting can mimic expensive, exotic materials successfully. Not only do you save money, but you can be environmentally conscious—all while creating something truly unique.

In this example, the finish is created with Chinese red and black oil glazes. The black glaze has been warmed with a small amount of burnt umber and phthalo blue; these colors are laid over a true red base coat of latex paint, then blended. Of course, the base coat must be thoroughly dry before glazing begins.

POSSIBLE VARIATIONS:
Use a green base coat and a dark-green glaze or a deep-blue base coat and a navy blue glaze.

How to Create Faux Morocco Leather

1 *Prepare the cheesecloth as described in the introduction (page 142). Mix the glaze to the desired color and thickness, and pour a little of it into the paint tray. Reseal the can to keep the solvent from evaporating.*

2 *Using a flat decorator brush on a small surface (or a roller on a large surface), lay the red glaze over 75 percent of the dry base coat. Apply it in broad, free-form strokes placed on the diagonal. Immediately lay the black glaze over 75 percent of the surface, using broad free-form strokes. This will leave about 5 percent of the base coat showing.*

3 With a bunched cheesecloth in hand, your partner should gently dab the surface with straight up-and-down strokes to blend the colors. If desired, he or she can do the blending with newsprint. (Follow the directions in step 2 on page 158.) This allows more of the base coat to show through.

4 The final finish. A stunning surface of great depth and sophistication that truly fools the eye.

F O R M U L A

CREATING FAUX MOROCCO LEATHER
(Negative Method 7)

SKILL LEVEL: Intermediate

RECOMMENDED FOR: Flat focal-point or accent walls

NOT RECOMMENDED FOR: Ceiling, floors, furniture, or any surface with intricate carving or elaborate trim

PAIRS OF HANDS NEEDED: 2

TOOLS: Painter's masking tape; paint buckets; mixing sticks; two paint trays; roller with low-nap or foam cover or 3-inch-wide flat decorator brush; 90-weight cheesecloth cut into 6-foot-long pieces; old newspapers; clean rags; mineral spirits; gloves

BASE COAT: Latex paint

GLAZE COLORANTS: Custom-mixed alkyd paint, universal tints, or artist's oil paints

GLAZE FORMULA: 1 part colorant, 1 part alkyd glazing medium, and 1 part mineral spirits

TYPICAL WORKABLE SECTION: A 2-foot-wide wall or surface

CLEAR TOP COAT: Optional

Of all the finishes, stippling is one of the few that has strictly utilitarian roots. For centuries, painters used it to even out and mask brush strokes on surfaces. The subtly grained matte texture produced by the method became so popular that eventually stippling was elevated to the lofty status of a decorative finish.

Stippling

Stippling involves pouncing a brush straight up and down over thin glaze to produce tiny pinpoints of color. Unlike some other decorative paint techniques, which either add or remove glaze to create texture, stippling pushes glaze into dots that allow the base coat to show through. It's a handsome effect, one that adds a rich accent to pale colors and intense, deep hues as well. Either way, a stippled finish enhances all types of surfaces, except those that are porous. It's an especially effective way to decorate furniture or trim.

Stippling, like the fine-art technique of pointillism, uses masses of tiny dots of paint that, from a distance, create the illusion of a single wash of color. Artist Lucianna Samu stippled the trim in this room.

For a good stippled finish, you should use a high-quality stippling brush with an even, consistent stroke. Professional stippling brushes can cost as much as $200. Don't fret; there are effective substitutes. You can make a wide, blocky stippling brush by taping together two ordinary and inexpensive staining brushes. A stiff-bristled scrub brush also works well for large surfaces, and a stiff-bristled artist's brush, a traditional stencil brush, or an oval sash brush easily handles small areas, especially if those areas feature intricate carvings or elaborate ornamentation.

Stippling involves a straight up-and-down pouncing stroke like that used for sponging, only you must work the brush a little more vigorously than you work the sponge. (See Chapter 6, "Sponging," page 128.) The more you stipple a surface, the lighter the color of the finish, and the more fine-grained the texture becomes.

All stippling calls for a latex base coat and an oil glaze to give you adequate working time. Don't use a latex glaze; it simply dries too fast, even if you add a drying retardant.

Stippling large surfaces definitely requires the efforts of two people, one to roll on the glaze and one to stipple it. Practice beforehand to discover how long you must wait after glazing before you can begin stippling and how large an area can be worked at one time; that way, one worker won't get too far ahead of the other. This experimenting also helps you to develop the consistently even stroke that stippling requires.

Professional stipplers are expensive, but you can substitute with an ordinary three-inch staining brush (left) or an oval sash brush (center), or tape together two extra-wide staining brushes (opposite) for large surfaces.

Stippling

- Basic Stippling

- Antique Stippling

- Antique Stippling: Three Colors

- Gradient Stippling: Two or More Colors

Basic Stippling

This is a good illustration of how stippling mellows a strong color by toning it down. It's also a way to grade together two different shades of one color or two entirely different colors. In this example, a bright-green base coat, which is thoroughly dry, is covered with a dark-green glaze that is tinted with black or raw umber, the green native color, and then worked with two sets of brush strokes: one rough and the other a fine stippling motion.

Masterstroke

For a subtle, sophisticated look, you can vary the technique. Apply two different colors to opposite ends of a surface. Leave a small area in the middle uncoated. Then take a cloth to work the glazes softly toward the center from each end until they overlap. With the stipple brush, you can further refine the finish, blending the colors so well that it will be impossible to perceive where one color ends and the other begins.

How to Stipple

1 Apply the base coat. In this case, it is a bright green, as shown. Let it dry. Mix the oil-based glaze to the desired color and thickness, and pour a small amount into a paint tray. Smoothly lay the glaze onto the first section using a roller.

2 Gripping the handle of a large, flat decorator brush as shown, your partner should immediately and quickly rough-stipple over the entire section using a pouncing stroke as described in the introduction (page 164). This begins pushing the glaze into tiny dots. Clean the brush frequently as you work.

3 For a fine stipple, work from side to side, pouncing a stippling brush over the entire surface as described in the introduction (page 164). Overlap the strokes as you go. To avoid creating a recognizable pattern, move your hand from side to side, and rotate the brush just before you make each stroke. Clean the brush frequently as you work.

4 The final finish: A deep color that has been mellowed and enriched by the addition of the stippled texture.

F O R M U L A

BASIC STIPPLING

SKILL LEVEL: Advanced beginner to intermediate

RECOMMENDED FOR: Almost all surfaces

NOT RECOMMENDED FOR: Porous surfaces

PAIRS OF HANDS NEEDED: 1 or 2, depending on the size of the surface

TOOLS: Paint buckets; mixing sticks; paint tray; roller with low-nap or foam cover; 3-inch-wide decorator brush; stippling brush; clean rags; mineral spirits; gloves

BASE COAT: Flat latex paint

GLAZE COLORANT: Custom-mixed flat, eggshell, or satin alkyd paint, universal tints, or artist's oil colors. Select sheened paint only if you want a shine in the final finish

GLAZE FORMULA: 1 part colorant, 1 part alkyd glazing medium, and 1 part mineral spirits

TYPICAL WORKABLE SECTION: A 2-foot-wide wall or surface

CLEAR TOP COAT: Optional

Antique Stippling

Stippling offers an excellent way to antique, or age, furniture and architectural elements such as fancy carved crown or cove molding, chair rails, and other trim. This simple negative technique involves pouncing the glaze on and wiping it off, leaving the flat areas almost clean and the detailed or raised areas accented. Trim treated in this way makes a fine accent for stippled walls.

Of course, wiping off the glaze doesn't just emphasize the molding's carving; it also highlights any imperfections in the stippled surface. You may or may not want these "character" lines to show. If you don't, be sure to repair the surface properly before painting. This means filling any holes, dents, or dings in the wood. If the surface has been previously painted or treated to any kind of finish, you should probably remove it. (See Chapter 4, "Surface Preparation: Building Your Base," beginning on page 79.)

Antique stippling looks best when it's executed with low-contrast colors. In this example, a slightly darker glaze is applied over a light base-coat color. An antiquing glaze, which is optional, was applied to add a hint of color.

How to Antique Stipple

1 Mix the glaze to the desired color and thickness, and pour a small amount into the paint tray. Reseal the can to keep the solvent from evaporating. Brush the glaze over the surface using a decorator brush, completely coating the area. If the trim has carved and plain areas as shown, apply the glaze only to the carved part at this point in the process.

2 Using an oval sash brush or other small brush, stipple the glaze with the stroke described in the introduction (page 164). This softens the glaze and adds working time to the technique. Stipple the area twice, but don't work it more than that, or you'll lighten the color too much.

3 *As the glaze begins to become matted, dampen a cheese-cloth pad with paint thinner, and wipe it along the molding, turning the pad so you're always working with a clean cloth.*

4 *If desired, apply a light coat of the antiquing glaze over the rest of the trim using a brush as shown. Feather out the glaze so that just a hint of color shows.*

5 *The finished trim. If desired, glaze the edge of the molding, and stipple it lightly so that color fades onto the wall.*

FORMULA

ANTIQUE STIPPLING

SKILL LEVEL: Advanced beginner to intermediate

RECOMMENDED FOR: High-relief or ornate surfaces such as moldings

NOT RECOMMENDED FOR: Flat surfaces

PAIRS OF HANDS NEEDED: 1

TOOLS: Paint buckets; mixing sticks; paint tray; 1½- to 2-inch-wide decorator brush; oval sash brush or other small stippling brush; 90-weight cheesecloth folded into pads; mineral spirits; gloves

BASE COAT: Eggshell or satin alkyd paint preferred, unless there's a preexisting latex finish on the molding

GLAZE COLORANT: Custom-mixed alkyd paint or universal tints toned down with a little raw umber artist's oil paint

GLAZE FORMULA: 1 part colorant, 1 part alkyd glazing medium, and 1 part mineral spirits

TYPICAL WORKABLE SECTION:
4 linear feet

CLEAR TOP COAT: No

Antique Stippling: Three Colors

This is a more decorative version of antique stippling with one color. It uses three closely related colors to create an elegant, subdued texture. It makes an excellent finish for such architectural elements as paneled doors, drawer fronts, trim, and any other surface where you want to accentuate the object's planes.

In this example, the finish is worked on a cabinet drawer front finished with a white cabinet epoxy. The beige, salmon-color, and green glazes have slightly more contrast than normal to emphasize the technique. The glazes are a 50-50 blend of custom-mixed satin alkyd paint and satin oil varnish. This glaze works well as a decorative finish onto wood with an existing finish. It flows on easily, adheres well, protects the surface, and lets you make touch-ups without redoing the entire piece. This glaze is also suitable for unpainted wood surfaces, but you must prime and paint them first.

You can dull the existing finish with a liquid deglosser, but do not sand it. Always wash the surface with a solution of trisodium phosphate (TSP).

How to Antique Stipple with Three Colors

1 *Mix the glazes to the desired colors and thicknesses. Pour a small amount of the first glaze into the paint tray. Reseal the cans to keep the solvents from evaporating. Brush the glaze onto the center panel. When it begins to approach snap time, stipple it with the pouncing stroke described in the introduction (page 164) until the glaze lightens to the desired color. Let the surface dry thoroughly.*

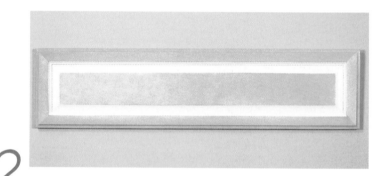

2 *Brush the second glaze onto the outside edges. When the glaze begins to approach snap time, stipple it with the same pouncing stroke that you made to stipple the center panel. Accent each mitered corner by laying a piece of sandpaper, grit side down, at a 45-degree angle along one side of it. Stipple over the sandpaper until the glaze lightens to the desired color. Let the surface dry.*

3 Mask the center panel and outside edges as shown. Apply the glaze to the beveled area. When it begins to approach snap time, stipple it until the glaze lightens to the desired color.

4 The finished appearance. As you can see, the stippled effect adds depth and texture to the drawer front. The look is more refined than a standard painted finish.

Masterstroke

If your home lacks architectural details such as ornamental trim, you can add it with prefabricated moldings made of wood or plastic. Both types can be finished with an antiqued stippling effect.

F O R M U L A

ANTIQUE STIPPLING: THREE COLORS

SKILL LEVEL: Intermediate

RECOMMENDED FOR: Surfaces with paneling, intricate carving, or elaborate trim

NOT RECOMMENDED FOR: Flat surfaces

PAIRS OF HANDS NEEDED: 1

TOOLS: Painter's masking tape; paper tape; paint buckets; mixing stick; paint tray; 2-inch-wide decorator brush; 80-grit sandpaper; oval sash brush; clean rags; mineral spirits; gloves

BASE COAT: Prefinished surface—existing finish cleaned with TSP solution or rubbed down with liquid deglosser. New surface—eggshell or satin alkyd paint over primer or sealer, as appropriate

GLAZE COLORANT: Custom-mixed satin alkyd paint or universal tints

GLAZE FORMULA: 1 part custom-mixed satin alkyd paint and 1 part satin oil varnish

TYPICAL WORKING SECTION: A 2-foot-wide surface

CLEAR TOP COAT: No

Gradient Stippling: Two or More Colors

This technique results in a more complex overall effect. It requires applying two or more tones of glaze in color blocks and blending them along their seams with a stippling brush. Keep stippling them until they seem to flow into and out of each other. Use one hue in different values and intensities to create a fade-away look; the example here uses contrasting colors that harmonize well and create dramatic shading. Either way, it's a smashing way to decorate walls in a large room where you can step back and observe the gradations of color.

The technique calls for dividing the wall into two or three horizontal sections, as appropriate. Apply the lightest color at the top and work down to the darkest color. When using only two contrasting colors, as shown here, divide the wall into two uneven sections to balance the space in favor of one color. Never divide a wall into even halves.

Don't forget to protect adjacent surfaces with painter's masking tape. To keep glaze from accumulating on the stippling brush, occasionally dab this brush into a bunched-up rag or onto old newspaper.

How to Gradient Stipple

1 *Mix the glazes to the desired colors and thicknesses. If using different values and intensities of one color, mix them as instructed for the variation on "Sponging On: Three Colors," pages 132–133. Pour a small amount of each glaze color into paint trays. Reseal the cans to keep the solvents from evaporating.*

2 *Using a roller, apply the glazes to the appropriate sections of the surface. Work from the top down, from the lightest to the darkest color.*

3 *Using a decorator brush, smooth the edges of the bands, and begin easing the glazes into one another. Start with the bottom band, and pull the glaze up 6 inches into the top or middle color. Pull the second color 6 inches down into the first color. Repeat along all the seams. Rough-stipple by pouncing the glazes with a decorator brush as described in the introduction, page 164. Start at the bottom, and work across the wall in horizontal sections. Pay particular attention to blurring the seams so that no color has a definite edge.*

4 Fine-stipple with a stippling brush. Again, start at the bottom, working across the wall in horizontal sections. Keep working to blur the color bands into each other.

5 The final finish. The finely grained texture and well-blended colors produce a filmy, misty look.

F O R M U L A

GRADIENT STIPPLING: TWO OR MORE COLORS

SKILL LEVEL: Advanced

RECOMMENDED FOR: Large, flat surfaces, especially walls

NOT RECOMMENDED FOR: Small areas, even if flat, and any surface with intricate carving or elaborate trim

PAIRS OF HANDS NEEDED: 1 or 2

TOOLS: Painter's masking tape; paint buckets; mixing sticks; paint trays; roller with low-nap or foam covers (one for each color glaze); 1½-inch- to 2-inch-wide flat decorator brush; stippling brush; clean rags; mineral spirits; gloves

BASE COAT: Eggshell or satin alkyd paint

GLAZE COLORANTS: Custom-mixed alkyd paints, universal tints, or artist's oil paints

GLAZE FORMULA: 1 part colorant, 1 part alkyd glazing medium, and 1 part mineral spirits

TYPICAL WORKABLE SECTION: A 2- or 3-foot-wide wall or surface

CLEAR TOP COAT: No; a clear topcoat would add too much depth to the color and mask the texture

Color washing, like stippling, has its roots in the past. However, unlike stippling, which first developed as a way to cover up surface flaws, color washing finds beauty in imperfection, and seeks to create it where it doesn't exist. Its rustic charm makes it an excellent choice for decorating walls in country-style and informal homes, as well as adding warmth to contemporary décors. It also presents a solution to the problem of painting a decorative finish on textured walls and ceilings. With color washing, you don't have to remove the texture or refinish the surface.

Color Washing

This technique calls for slapping on layers of thin glaze and blending them to produce the same faded, uneven look of walls painted with distemper or whitewash. The result depends on the type of glaze and the tool that applies it.

Color washing is a versatile technique that can be applied to smooth or textured walls and ceilings. The oil glaze used to color-wash this ceiling gives the room a warm glow.

Latex glazes work as well as oil glazes in this instance because you'll be working so fast that drying time usually isn't a serious concern. However, because you're using a thin glaze, you may want to work with a partner who can brush out drips and runs the instant they occur. A wash of diluted paint also works well.

Thinned paints and latex glazes produce an almost sheer but slightly opaque effect. Understand that when you thin latex paint, you don't make it transparent as such; you simply put more space between the molecules of pigment. An oil glaze, however, produces a translucent effect that gives off a warm glow and greater depth than its latex counterpart, which can appear flatter and less light-reflective.

As for application tools, you have a choice among brushes, sponges, and cloth. Cloth produces the softest effect, but a wide brush lets you work quite quickly. Many times you will use all three tools in one project.

When color washing walls, be sure to mask adjoining surfaces in the corners, at the ceiling, along the baseboards, and around all door and window trim. (See "Protecting Adjoining Surfaces," page 143.)

A sponge, a brush, or cloth may be used to color-wash a wall or surface. Don't be afraid to use all three.

When you're considering colors for the glazes, the rule of thumb concerning color washing is that this decorative finish works best when it puts a pale glaze over a pale base coat, with all the hues coming from the same color family or analogous ones. Applying light glazes over dark base coats can produce sophisticated effects; however, beginners do best working with pale colors that create low contrast.

Color washing is a free-form, kinetic art. Beginners, forgetting this fact, make the mistake of holding back and not going far enough with it. As with many of the decorative paint finishes, don't let yourself get so focused on one section of wall that you forget to step back frequently to see the wall—and the effect—as a whole.

In many ways, color washing is closely related to sponging, so take time to review Chapter 6, "Sponging," beginning on page 126, before you start.

Color Washing

- Color Washing: One Color

- Color Washing: Two Colors

- French-Brush Color Washing

Color Washing: One Color

It actually helps to apply your finish over a base coat of a slightly textured surface, which gives the glaze something to grab. In this example, a flat latex glaze is worked over a flat latex base coat to produce a soft, muted wall with just a hint of texture on its surface. The texture comes from first blending the glaze with a sponge and then blending it with a brush worked in loose figure-eight strokes.

Masterstroke

Because a wash is basically watered-down glaze, it gives you the freedom to be more adventuresome with your color selection. Although beginners may want to play it safe with pale hues, there really is no harm done by trying the more sophisticated approach of applying a vivid, rich hue, which, in its diluted state, will look much less intense. If you don't like the result, you can simply sponge over it (once it dries) with a paler shade of the same color.

How to Color Wash

1 *Mix the glaze to the desired color and thickness. Make it thin but not runny. Pour a small amount into the paint tray. Reseal the can to prevent spills.*

2 *Use a brush or a roller to lay the glaze over the base coat, applying it with three sets of crisscross strokes. First, apply vertical strokes, from top to bottom; second, use horizontal strokes, from side to side; and third, make vertical strokes, from top to bottom. This sets up the glaze.*

3 *Immediately break up the glaze by texturing it with a slightly damp sponge. Lightly drag, roll, and dab the sponge*

over the surface. Clean the sponge as often as necessary to keep it from becoming saturated with glaze.

4 Using a dry staining brush, immediately smooth out the remaining glaze with alternating figure-eight strokes, barely touching the surface so you don't create brush marks. This blends the strokes and folds the texture into the glaze.

5 The final finish. Completing the project by lightly working the glaze with a dry brush gives the wall a rustic look.

F O R M U L A

COLOR WASHING: ONE COLOR

SKILL LEVEL: Intermediate

RECOMMENDED FOR: All large, flat walls, including those with textured surfaces; floors; tabletops; and countertops

NOT RECOMMENDED FOR: Ceilings, small objects, or surfaces with intricate carving or elaborate trim

PAIRS OF HANDS NEEDED: 1 to 3, depending on the size of the surface

TOOLS: Painter's masking tape; paint buckets; mixing sticks; paint tray; 3-inch-wide decorator brush or roller with low-nap or foam cover; staining brush; sea sponge; buckets of clean water to clean sponge; stain brush; clean rags; gloves

BASE COAT: Latex paint

GLAZE COLORANT: Custom-mixed flat latex paint, artist's acrylics, or universal tints

GLAZE FORMULA: 1 part colorant, 1 part acrylic glazing medium, 2 to 3 parts water

TYPICAL WORKABLE SECTION: A 2-foot-wide wall or surface

CLEAR TOP COAT: Optional

Color Washing: Two Colors

This is the method of color washing with which people are most familiar. It involves using oil glazes; because you'll be applying more than one color, you need more time to complete the work. Latex paints dry too quickly for this process.

This technique, which is worked using a sponge, produces a glowing, cloudlike effect and a softness that also has immense depth. For the best result, keep the two glaze colors closely related. In this example, two shades of blue—one close to true blue and a different, gray-blue version—are applied over a cool-white base coat of flat latex paint. The base coat should be thoroughly dry before you begin glazing.

How to Color Wash with Two Colors

1 *Mix the glazes to the desired colors and thicknesses. Make them watery but not so thin that they run. Pour a small amount of each color into paint trays. Reseal the cans to keep the solvent from evaporating.*

2 *Wash the lightest color glaze over the wall using a damp sponge, and working diagonally across the wall. Keep your strokes loose, and apply them at random. Cover about 60 percent of the wall's surface. Step back and check your work. The strokes should be balanced across the section with about 40 percent of the base-coat color showing through at this point.*

3 *Using a new damp sponge and the same stroking technique, immediately wash the darker glaze over the wall. Apply some of the strokes over the first glaze and some over the exposed base coat. About 15 percent of the base coat shows through when you've completed this step.*

4 Immediately blend the colors with another clean, damp sponge. Use the same light figure-eight stroke used in Step 4 of "Color Washing: One Color," page 179. This stroke should barely touch the surface. Keep working until you take the color back to the desired degree of softness.

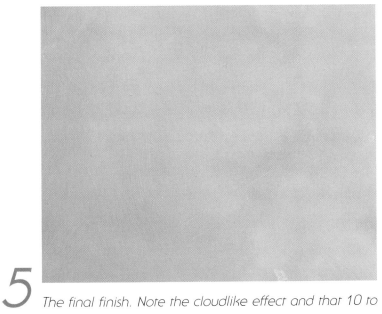

5 The final finish. Note the cloudlike effect and that 10 to 15 percent of the white base color shows through.

F O R M U L A

COLOR WASHING: TWO COLORS

SKILL LEVEL: Intermediate

RECOMMENDED FOR: All large, flat walls, including textured walls; ceilings, including textured ceilings; floors; tabletops; and countertops

NOT RECOMMENDED FOR: Any small surfaces or surfaces with intricate carving or elaborate trim

PAIRS OF HANDS NEEDED: 1 to 3, depending on the size of the surface

TOOLS: Painter's masking tape; paint buckets; mixing sticks; 2 paint trays; 2 to 4 sea sponges; clean rags; mineral spirits; gloves

BASE COAT: Flat latex paint

GLAZE COLORANT: Custom-mixed alkyd paint, universal tints, or artist's oil paints

GLAZE FORMULA: 1 part colorant, 1 part alkyd glazing medium, and 2 to 3 parts mineral spirits

TYPICAL WORKABLE SECTION: A 2-foot-wide wall or surface

CLEAR TOP COAT: Optional. If desired, use a matte-finish top coat

French-Brush Color Washing

This finish calls for applying and working paint (not glaze) using a brush. It's the only color-washing technique that uses full-bodied paint and skips glazing. It produces a mottled, aged texture that makes it the most forgiving of the color-washing techniques; it's easy to touch up if you make a mistake or skip a spot.

French brushing always looks best when executed in a subtle color range. In this example, three colors of paint—a warm white, a light orange, and a medium orange—are applied over a coat of warm-white primer.

You can use undiluted paint taken straight from the can, or you can loosen the paint slightly by adding 10 percent water. Because the first coat is a warm-white latex paint, you don't have to apply a base coat. You can also start with the wall covered with nothing but a white primer or sealer.

Keep the surface wet to the end. That's the key to success with this finish. Because you'll use flat latex paint, you may want help. Otherwise, add extenders to the paint, or keep wetting the brush.

How to French-Brush a Color Wash

1 *If creating your own colors, mix the paints to the desired hues. Thin them by adding 10 percent water if desired, but don't let them become watery or runny. Pour a small amount of each color into the paint trays. Reseal the cans to prevent spills.*

2 *Working at a 45-degree angle across the surface, slap the white latex paint all over the surface using a decorator brush and moving in short, random strokes. Don't be afraid to let the primer or base color show through.*

 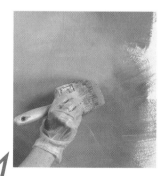

3 *Working the same way and with the same brush, immediately slap on the lightest paint color.*

4 *Promptly follow this coat with the darkest color. Using a new brush, cover some of the other paints.*

5 Using the white latex paint and the brush with which you applied it in Step 2, slap a few strokes of the paint at random over the entire surface. Using a new brush and working at a 45-degree angle, smooth and blend the colors. Barely touch the surface with the tip of the brush. You can do this with loose figure-eight strokes, if you wish. Continue working until you get the desired mottled effect, but remember: The more you work the paint, the more you'll blend and lighten the colors.

6 The final finish: a misty, mottled texture. As you create this finish, don't let small defects or mistakes bother you. They'll disappear into the overall effect.

F O R M U L A

FRENCH-BRUSH COLOR WASHING

SKILL LEVEL: Intermediate to advanced

RECOMMENDED FOR: All large walls, including those with textured surfaces; ceilings, including those with texture; floors; tabletops; and countertops

NOT RECOMMENDED FOR: Small surfaces, or any surface with intricate carving or elaborate trim

PAIRS OF HANDS NEEDED: 1 to 3, depending on project's size

TOOLS: Painter's masking tape; paint buckets; 3 paint trays; 3 2½-inch-wide decorator brushes; bucket of clean water for wetting down the surface; sponge; clean rags; gloves

BASE COAT: A coat of sealer or primer or, if desired, flat latex paint

PAINT: Custom-mixed flat latex paints, or mix your own with universal tints or artist's acrylics. Use full-bodied paint or thin with 10 percent water if desired

TYPICAL WORKING SECTION: A 2-foot-wide wall or surface

CLEAR TOP COAT: Optional

Put simply, spattering is a random method of applying color. When you think of spattering, you may recall the art projects you made in grammar school. It's true that this is an elementary technique, but it can also be a sophisticated one that bears little resemblance to the paint splashes your mother lovingly displayed on the refrigerator door.

Spattered finishes run the gamut from brightly colored paint flecks that display a bold blend of color, to soft watermark effects created by specks of thinner, to complex finishes that resemble semiprecious stones such as lapis lazuli. Whatever the look, spattering offers an excellent way to decorate everything from furnishings to walls. Positive spattering, especially, looks incredibly simple to do. In one way it is, but it also requires thought, planning, a consistent stroke, and plenty of time.

Spattering in a even, balanced manner is no small feat. This is especially true for large surfaces such as walls.

The standard method for spattering involves loading a spattering brush (an oval sash brush will do fine) with paint or glaze and tapping the side of the brush's ferrule against a stick or another brush handle so that tiny dots of color spray over a surface. An equally common process entails loading a stiff-bristled brush with paint or glaze and running a palette knife, tongue depressor, or your thumb over the bristles. This sends a shower of tiny colored droplets over the surface. Running a toothbrush over a paint screen does the same thing, providing an ideal way to spatter small surfaces—a picture frame, for example. (You'll also need a natural sponge to pounce on or lift off some of the glazes.)

Reviewing all of these methods raises a question: Why not use an air gun or paint sprayer? You certainly can. Although these power tools do the job quickly and let you

Masterstroke

The more layers to your painted design, the more complex and sophisticated it becomes. Try this: Over the base coat, apply a negative sponging technique. Once it dries, stencil a pattern or border on the wall or surface. (See Chapter 13, "Stenciling," page 207.) Let that dry, and then spatter over your design with one or two soft colors.

control the force with which the paint or glaze sprays onto the wall, you must still trigger the flow and control the movement over the surface. And you have to properly mask adjacent areas or surfaces to protect them from residual drops of paint flying through the air. If you want to use a sprayer, rent a unit and practice—then practice some more. It's not as easy to use as you may think.

All spattering methods make a mess. You should cover everything in sight that you don't want spattered, including yourself, before starting the project.

The final result depends on many things: choice of color, paint and glaze thickness, and the rhythm of the strokes. Prepare a glaze of medium consistency, so the paint sprays on in fine flecks rather than blobs or blotches. Before you attempt a big project—and after you experiment and practice to your heart's content—carry several small projects to completion. This testing period will help you determine how far away you must stand from a surface to produce dots of different sizes. The distance factor is important because some projects require an even dot size throughout, while others call for a variety of sizes.

Spattering

- Spattering On:
  Four Colors

- Spattering Off

The furry side of a natural sponge (right) and a spattering brush (opposite) are tools used to create the effect.

Spattering On: Four Colors

Spattering on creates beautiful texture with amazing depth. Sometimes it's used as an antiquing effect. In this example, it captures the stunning beauty of polished lapis lazuli. This look calls for a blue base coat spattered with dark blue, blue, white, and gold latex glazes of medium consistency. However, you can use any color combination you want; the possibilities are endless.

Unlike many other decorative painting techniques, spattering uses a full-bodied latex paint for some of its glaze. Thin the paint with a little water to loosen it, but don't let it become runny. This consistency easily shakes off the brush in fine flecks or dots. Also, full-bodied paint provides the opacity needed for the dots to stand out from the base-coat color.

Start with a thoroughly dry base coat—in this example, a handsome medium-blue flat latex paint. It works well for small sections of walls and most accessories; for furniture, use an eggshell latex as the base coat. Spattering produces a slightly raised surface, which may not be appealing on furniture. In that case, level the finish with several coats of varnish.

How to Spatter On Four Colors

1   Cover all adjoining surfaces. Mix the latex glaze to the desired color and thickness. Pour a small amount into the paint tray, and reseal the can. Using a roller or paintbrush, cover the base coat with the glaze.

2   Using the furry side of a sponge and the stroke described in "Sponging," page 129, pounce the surface, picking up about 50 percent of the glaze. Let the surface dry.

3   Thin the paint with water. Load the brush, shake off the excess, and then strike its ferrule against a stick. Spatter 40 percent of the surface, and let it dry. Repeat this with the second coat, letting about 40 percent of the base coat show through. Let it dry.

4 Repeat Step 3 with the third spatter coat. Let about 30 percent of the base-coat color show through. Let it dry, and then repeat Step 3, using a slightly thinned gold latex paint. Keep this last coat sparse so that the gold creates only an accent. Let the entire surface dry.

5 The final finish. The random but balanced arrangement of the colored dots creates a sense of immense depth and mystery. Applying a clear top coat with a glossy finish deepens the color and adds a nice sheen.

FORMULA

SPATTERING ON: FOUR COLORS

SKILL LEVEL: Beginner to intermediate

RECOMMENDED FOR: Small and medium-size surfaces, such as accent walls, furniture, and accessories

NOT RECOMMENDED FOR: Ceilings or other large, flat surfaces

PAIRS OF HANDS REQUIRED: 1

TOOLS: Masking tape; drop cloths; paint buckets; mixing sticks; paint tray; roller with low-nap cover or paintbrush properly sized to surface; sea sponge; 4 spattering brushes; wooden stick; clean rags; water

BASE COAT: Flat latex paint

GLAZE COLORANTS: Custom-mixed flat or eggshell latex paints, artist's acrylics, or universal tints

GLAZE FORMULA: First glaze coat—1 part colorant, 1 part latex glazing medium, and 1 part water. Other glaze coats— custom-mixed latex paints slightly thinned by adding 10 percent water

TYPICAL WORKABLE SECTION: A 2-foot-wide surface or wall

CLEAR TOP COAT: Optional

Spattering Off

This negative method involves spattering mineral spirits over a surface covered with a transparent oil glaze in order to produce the look of watered silk. The trick is to add the solvent at the right moment when the glaze just begins to mat down, a sign that it's approaching snap time. (Use white mineral spirits or paint thinner—essentially the same product—rather than kerosene or turpentine because it does a better job of opening up the surface.)

You may want to work with a partner, but this technique looks best on small or medium-size surfaces, which you may be able to handle by yourself. Another tip: Use base-coat and oil-glaze colors that are from the same color family and are only slightly different in tone. In this example, a gray oil glaze goes over a paler gray, flat latex base coat. The glaze is just an alkyd paint thinned with solvent. You can also work with latex paint and glaze, in which case you should spatter with denatured alcohol. Work quickly, because the alcohol reacts to elements in the base coat.

How to Spatter Off

1 Mix a thin oil glaze to the desired color and thickness. Make it very translucent. Pour a small amount into the paint tray. Reseal the can to prevent the solvent from evaporating.

2 Using a sponge, apply the glaze to the surface, making your strokes at a 45-degree angle. Then, using the pouncing stroke described in the introduction to Chapter 6, "Sponging," page 129, texture the glaze with the sponge. Let the glaze stand until it just begins to mat down and becomes sticky.

3 Spatter the surface with mineral spirits, using the spattering technique described in the introduction (page 186), and then

carefully pull off the thinner with a chamois cloth bunched up in your hand. Hold the chamois, and stroke it in the manner described in the introduction to "Sponging," page 129. Be selective about how hard you press, and don't move the chamois around on the surface. You want to remove the thinner and just enough of the glaze to create a watermark effect. Let the surface dry.

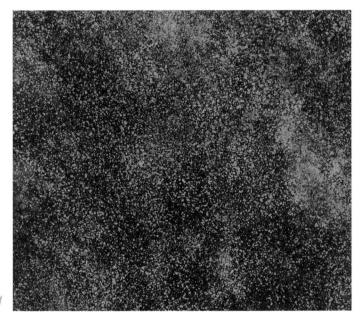

4 The final finish. If desired, apply an overglaze the next day. Spatter it on the surface, and pick it up with bunched cheesecloth using the technique described in the introduction to "Ragging," page 142. Dry the overglaze with an electric blow dryer. Complete with a clear top coat to deepen the color.

F O R M U L A

SPATTERING OFF

SKILL LEVEL: Advanced beginner to intermediate

RECOMMENDED FOR: Small and medium-size surfaces, including accent walls, furniture, architectural elements, and accessories

NOT RECOMMENDED FOR: Ceilings, floors, or large surfaces

PAIRS OF HANDS NEEDED: 1 or 2, as desired

TOOLS: Masking tape; paint buckets; mixing sticks; paint tray; sea sponges; spattering brush; chamois cloth; clean rags; mineral spirits; gloves; electric blow dryer

BASE COAT: Flat or eggshell latex paint

GLAZE COLORANT: Custom-mixed eggshell alkyd paint, universal tints, or artist's oils

GLAZE FORMULA: 1 part colorant to 1 part mineral spirits. No alkyd glazing medium

OVERGLAZE FORMULA: 1 part colorant to 9 parts solvent

TYPICAL WORKABLE SECTION: A 3-foot-square area

CLEAR TOP COAT: Yes

CHAPTER 11

Combing

Sometimes called *dragging*, this technique is also known as *strié* because of its linear pattern. In the context of decorative painting, combing refers to marking narrow lines of color on a surface. It's a classic method for softening or accenting any surface with subtle nuances of color, and it has been used for this purpose for centuries—it probably grew out of the original wood-graining techniques. It makes an especially pretty finish for trim and painted paneling.

A negative technique, combing calls for dragging a tool through a translucent glaze, removing some of the glaze, and giving the surface a set of controlled marks. Usually they're fine vertical marks, but they can be horizontal, diagonal, or curved, and either bold or fine.

The charm of combing is in the unevenness of the lines and the variations in designs. This room features a combed basket-weave pattern on the upper portion of the wall.

Whatever the shape of the lines, you make them by lifting off glaze using a tool—a pad of steel wool, a stiff-bristle brush, a notched squeegee, a graining comb, a grooming comb, a piece of cardboard, or whatever else is handy. This chapter reviews combed patterns made using three of the most common tools: steel-wool pads, a brush, and a notched squeegee.

When your aim is to create a combed, plaited, or crosshatched pattern, you want lines that are, if not perfect, at least reasonably straight. This presents two challenges: making truly plumb or level lines and making each stroke continuous from top to bottom. Whatever tool you use, work it so that the strokes run straight up and down or straight across the surface. That's just about impossible to do freehand, especially on large surfaces, which means you need some type of accurate but inconspicuous guidelines to follow. Either snap plumb lines at sensible intervals across the surface using a chalk-line box loaded with light-colored chalk (hoping the combing process covers up the lines), or use a carpenter's spirit level as a guide, and put up long pieces of masking tape to follow.

If you don't want to make too many lines on the surface and you have *extremely* good hand-eye coordination, hold a carpenter's level on the wall, and pull the combing tool parallel with it using your free hand. Put down the level, and make the next few strokes freehand by aligning the comb's edge with a dark or light line in the guide stroke. After a few strokes, hold the level in place again, and

A stiff-bristle brush, a notched squeegee, or steel wool are a few of the tools that may be dragged through wet glaze to create a combed effect.

make another guide stroke parallel to it. Continue in this manner until the entire surface has been marked. For small surfaces, it may be possible to make straight lines simply by sighting along the object's edge.

Whatever method you use, stop after a few strokes to check the straightness of your lines. They don't have to be perfect, but they should be close to it.

Usually you'll want a continuous combed line. That means you can't stop in the middle of a stroke—you must keep moving the tool, whether from top to bottom or side to side. This is difficult to do on a large surface such as a wall. It helps to work with a partner to whom you can hand off the tool when you come to the end of your reach. Also, use a stepladder when combing a wall vertically. Step down the ladder and then off at the bottom to keep the strokes moving from top to bottom.

Combing

- **Combing with Steel-Wool**

- **Combing with a Hard-Bristle Brush**

- **Combing with a Notched Squeegee**

Combing calls for putting a tinted, almost transparent glaze over a low-contrast base coat. Typical combinations include a pale glaze over a white or neutral base, or a deeper but highly translucent glaze over a pastel base drawn from the same color family. Both combinations produce a tone-on-tone look. More color combinations are possible, but they take careful coordination. Also, subtle color contrasts produce a lustrous, luminous finish with the beauty of silk. The more contrast you have between the base coat and glaze, the more prominent the stripes become and mistakes or imperfections show. You may want to wait to do this when you have more experience.

Use latex or alkyd paint for the base coat, as you prefer, but always use a thick oil glaze over it for combing. This glaze gives you the translucency and the working time you need for a successful project. However, for combing trim molding with an existing enamel finish, make a special glaze by mixing a few drops of colorant into a satin-finish oil varnish.

Combing with Steel Wool

Dragging a pad of steel wool through a glaze produces a finely textured surface. First, you'll have to apply the glaze by using three sets of strokes: vertical, horizontal, then vertical again, in a crisscross pattern. Combing over the glaze with the steel-wool pad adds a textural quality. It's an attractive finish for woodwork and paneling. In this example, a warm-white base coat receives a burnt-sienna oil glaze that you comb using pads of #00 steel wool.

Masterstroke

If it is too difficult to make one interrupted stroke, start at the top, and drag the pad down as far below eye level as you can go. Feather the stroke out. Then from the bottom up to the edge of your previous stroke, drag the pad up. Feather out the area where the two strokes meet. To camouflage further, stagger the intersecting points of all the vertical and horizontal strokes made this way.

How to Comb with Steel Wool

1 Mix the glaze to the desired color and thickness, and pour a small amount into the paint tray. Reseal the can to keep the solvent from evaporating.

2 Using a roller, lay the glaze evenly over the surface with a set of three crisscross strokes: first, work from top to bottom; second, from side to side; third, from top to bottom again. This sets up the glaze and creates a subtexture.

3 Hold a steel-wool pad at a 45-degree angle, as shown. Only its edge should touch the surface. Drag it straight down through the glaze. This is one time you don't need to make continuous strokes from top to bottom. Feather the pad as you approach the bottom of the wall so that you don't create an identifiable solid line. Keep turning and wiping off the pad as you work. When the pad becomes too loaded with glaze, discard it and use a new one. Be sure to keep a wet edge.

4 Stop frequently to check your work with a ruler or a carpenter's spirit level. You want to make sure you have reasonably straight strokes. Remove about 50 percent of the glaze as you work. Let the surface dry.

5 The final finish: A finely textured surface that resembles raw silk. About 50 percent of the base-coat color shows through. The wall seems to glow with luminous color.

F O R M U L A

COMBING WITH STEEL WOOL

SKILL LEVEL: Advanced beginner to intermediate

RECOMMENDED FOR: All flat surfaces, large or small

NOT RECOMMENDED FOR: Any surface with intricate carving or elaborate trim

PAIRS OF HANDS NEEDED: 1 or 2, as desired

TOOLS: Ruler or carpenter's spirit level; #1 pencil or chalk-line box with plumb bob and light-colored chalk; painters' masking tape; mixing sticks; paint buckets; paint tray; roller with low-nap or foam cover; #00 steel wool pads; clean rags; mineral spirits; gloves

BASE COAT: Flat latex paint (Eggshell latex paint offers a more graphic texture, but flat latex is easier for a beginner to use.)

GLAZE COLORANT: Custom-mixed alkyd paint or universal tints

GLAZE FORMULA: 1 part colorant, 1 part alkyd glazing medium, and a little less than 1 part mineral spirits to make a thick glaze

TYPICAL WORKABLE SECTION: A 2- to 3-foot-wide wall or surface

CLEAR TOP COAT: Optional

Combing with a Hard-Bristle Brush

This traditional method of combing produces a deep, lustrous finish. It calls for a very translucent oil glaze that's several tones darker than the base coat. Pull a stiff-bristled brush through the glaze to remove some of the glaze and create fine stripes. The technique works best when the base coat and glaze are close in color.

How to Comb with a Hard-Bristle Brush

1 Mix the glaze to the desired color and thickness, and pour a small amount into the paint tray. Reseal the can to keep the solvent from evaporating.

2 Brush the glaze onto the wall using three sets of crisscross strokes: first, from top to bottom; second, from side to side; and third, from top to bottom again. This sets up the glaze.

A combed painted-plaid effect is simple and involves contrasting shades. To recreate the look shown, apply the base coat, let it dry, and then make a grid using strips of narrow masking tape. Brush on glaze in a series of evenly spaced wide vertical stripes; pull a clean brush through the wet glaze. Next brush on a deeper shade of the same-color glaze in a series of evenly spaced horizontal stripes to create a crossbarred pattern; pull a clean brush through this new coat of wet glaze. Remove the masking tape once the glaze completely dries.

3 *Press a clean decorator brush flat against the wall, as shown, and pull it down through the glaze in a continuous stroke. Work from top to bottom. Do this one time in each spot, wiping the brush clean after each stroke. Be sure to keep a wet edge.*

4 *The final finish. For a finely combed finish, make one set of strokes. For a rougher effect, comb the surface with a second set of brush strokes.*

FORMULA

COMBING WITH A HARD-BRISTLE BRUSH

SKILL LEVEL: Advanced beginner to intermediate

RECOMMENDED FOR: Flat, small to medium-size surfaces, either vertical or horizontal

NOT RECOMMENDED FOR: Ceilings, large surfaces, or surfaces with intricate carving or elaborate molding

PAIRS OF HANDS NEEDED: 1

TOOLS: Chalk-line box with plumb bob and light-colored chalk or carpenter's level; painter's masking tape; paint buckets;, paint tray; several 3-inch-wide decorator brushes; clean rags; mineral spirits; gloves

BASE COAT: Latex paint

GLAZE COLORANT: Custom-mixed alkyd paint, universal tints, or artist's oils

GLAZE FORMULA: 1 part colorant, 1 part alkyd glazing medium, and a little less than 1 part mineral spirits to make a thick glaze

TYPICAL WORKABLE SECTION: A 2- to 3-foot-wide wall or surface

CLEAR TOP COAT: Optional

Combing with a Notched Squeegee

Not all strokes must run straight up and down. Make them freeform, horizontal or diagonal, curved or straight, and as bold or as fine as you wish. All it takes is a squeegee notched to the desired pattern. Use a pair of scissors or craft knife to notch the squeegee with a freehand pattern, or measure and cut a precise pattern if you like. The texture and pattern that result make a pleasing graphic design.

You can also use graining combs and pipe grainers if you have these tools on hand; a plastic hair brush can also substitute.

Mount the squeegee on a 2-foot extension pole, which will allow you to step back from the surface as you drag the tool through the glaze. This makes it easier to create reasonably straight strokes as well as continuous ones; however, you can pause between strokes if you must. Be sure to clean the squeegee after each pass. Again, the safest strategy is keep the color contrast low, as in the examples, until you are proficient.

How to Comb with a Notched Squeegee

1   *Notch the squeegee with your chosen pattern. Mix the glaze to the desired color and thickness, and pour a small amount into the paint tray. Reseal the can.*

2   *Brush or roll the glaze onto the surface with three sets of crisscross strokes: first, from top to bottom; second, from side to side; third, from top to bottom again. This sets up the glaze and gives it a subtexture.*

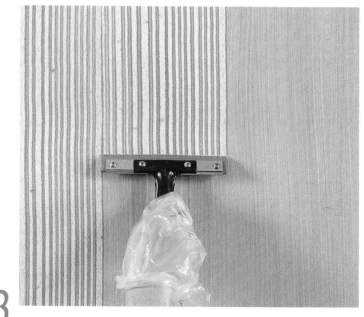

3   *Set the squeegee against the surface at a 45-degree angle, as shown, and pull straight down through the glaze in a continuous stroke. Keep steady pressure on the squeegee as you pull. As you begin each new stroke, align the end of the squeegee with the outermost drag mark in the previous stroke. Let the surface dry.*

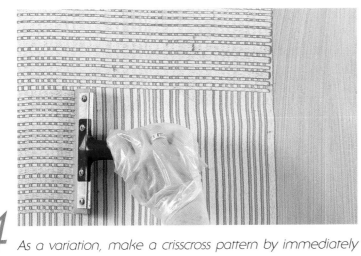

4 As a variation, make a crisscross pattern by immediately pulling horizontal strokes across the vertical strokes, as shown. The vertical strokes show through as a subtexture. Let the surface dry.

5 Some alternative patterns include (clockwise from top left) crisscross, basket weave, free form, and curved lines.

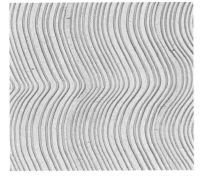

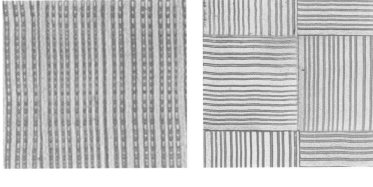

FORMULA

COMBING WITH A NOTCHED SQUEEGEE

SKILL LEVEL: Intermediate

RECOMMENDED FOR: Small to medium-size surfaces that are flat and smooth

NOT RECOMMENDED FOR: Ceilings, large surfaces, or any surface with intricate carving or elaborate trim

PAIRS OF HANDS NEEDED: At least 2

TOOLS: Carpenter's spirit level; chalk-line box with light-colored chalk; paint buckets; paint tray; mixing stick; roller with low-nap or foam cover or 3-inch-wide decorator brush; scissors or craft knife; notched squeegee or graining comb; squeegee extension pole if desired; clean rags; mineral spirits; gloves

BASE COAT: Flat latex paint

GLAZE COLORANT: Custom-mixed alkyd paint, universal tints, or artist's oils

GLAZE FORMULA: 1 part colorant, 1 part alkyd glazing medium, and a little less than 1 part mineral spirits to make a thick glaze

TYPICAL WORKABLE SECTION: A 2-foot-wide wall or surface

CLEAR TOP COAT: Optional

Can you imagine a more pleasant decorative illusion than a blue sky with billowy clouds? This *trompe l'oeil* finish produces intriguing walls and splendid ceilings. (*Trompe l'oeil*, French for "fool the eye," describes a painting that mimics something so well it looks real.) Although *trompe l'oeil* effects usually require the skill of an artist, a painted sky is easy to accomplish and attractive. It is executed using a dry brush, much the same as French-brush color washing—the chief difference being the use of full-bodied latex paint straight from the can instead of a thin glaze. The key to success is keeping the surface wet to the end, which means you must work quickly. To begin, coat the surface with a warm-white flat latex paint, and let it dry. Just two colors achieve a basic but effective version of the look.

Creating a Sky Effect

All you need is two colors—*a vibrant sky blue and off-white—to achieve a basic but effective version of the sky effect.*

Creating a Sky Effect

A painted sky can appear soft and pretty in a baby's nursery, but it can also look highly sophisticated in other rooms of the house. It all depends on the rest of the furnishings and whether or not you choose a complex blend of colors for your rendering. (See the Masterstroke, below.) Start it halfway up the walls, and progress the effect onto the ceiling to visually dissolve the confines of the room. Just remember that although the basic application of the technique is easy, painting overhead can be tedious and may require some kind of scaffolding.

Masterstroke

Once you get the hang of the basic blue-and-white application, try a more complex rendering of sky. Instead of a white base coat, try a creamy pale yellow, which will look like sunshine peeking through the clouds. Use a range of colors— several shades of blue, for example, or deep purples, greens, and grays for shading. For better blending, stipple the colors until there are no hard edges.

How to Paint a Sky

1 Once the base coat dries, apply the blue sky paint with a brush or roller. Let it dry. Then working at a 45-degree angle, slap white paint over the surface using short, random strokes from a 4-inch-wide decorator brush, as shown. Pull the paint out until it's thin in some areas, and overlay it in others so that you create an uneven color overall. If you wish, imitate the color gradation found in the sky by leaving the tops of walls and the centers of ceilings more blue.

2 Work the paint so that it has this mottled effect. This mottling begins to suggest where you should place the clouds.

3 Use a dry 2-inch-wide decorator brush tipped with the white paint to establish cloud shapes in the light sections. Use random, flowing strokes (as shown here) to smooth and blend the two colors. Be loose, and don't think of cloud shapes as such; your goal is to create billowy shapes with a mottled effect. Follow up by adding more blue with a brush wherever you feel it's needed to create the right balance. Let the surface dry.

4 The final finish. To complete the finish, mix 8 parts water with 1 part white paint to make a thin wash. Brush this wash over the entire surface, and let it dry. It has a softening effect that breaks up the blue and pulls everything together.

F O R M U L A

CREATING A SKY EFFECT

SKILL LEVEL: Advanced intermediate to advanced

RECOMMENDED FOR: Large flat surfaces like walls and smooth ceilings

NOT RECOMMENDED FOR: Floors or any surface with intricate carving or elaborate trim

PAIRS OF HANDS NEEDED: 1

TOOLS: Paint buckets; paint tray; mixing sticks; roller; 4-inch-wide decorator brush; 2-inch-wide decorator brush; bucket of clean water; clean rags; gloves

BASE COAT: Warm-white flat latex paint

FINISH FORMULA: Custom-mixed flat latex paint in blue and warm off-white

OVERGLAZE: 1 part off-white flat latex paint and 8 parts water

TYPICAL WORKING SECTION: A 2-foot-wide wall or ceiling.

CLEAR TOP COAT: No

When you think of stenciling, the words *simple*, *versatile*, *structured*, *stylized*, and *decorative* should come to mind. This easy means for adding patterns to a wall, floor, furniture, or fabric is merely the process of repeating one motif over and over again. And there is much more to this traditional art form than the Colonial or folk motifs with which it is so strongly associated in this country.

Stenciling

Stenciling can be traced back through an ancient and honorable history. Examples are found in the Egyptian pyramids and in Pompeian villas, as well as in many Early American homes. Stenciling also has contemporary forms with roots in the technique's revival in the Arts and Crafts, Art Nouveau, and Art Deco movements at the turn of the twentieth century. It's experiencing another strong renaissance as we begin a new century.

Stenciling *can be used as a way to apply architectural motifs or other painted decoration to a surface. A stenciled palm tree on the wall next to the bath adds an exotic oasislike feeling to the room.*

The stencil pattern *painted on this floor was designed to mimic the ceramic-tile backsplash.*

Don't be afraid to expand your ideas to painting a field of patterns on your walls and other surfaces, including wood floors, floor coverings, furniture, fabric, and accessories. Wherever you can put paint, you can stencil a design. Stenciled motifs range from simple to complex, as do the color schemes with which you can apply them. Stencils are usually executed with one or two colors, but there are some complex stencil patterns created with as many as 25 colors. However, such intricate designs may become overwhelming if you have to do them by yourself. They take a tremendous amount of time to apply, and their very complexity makes them confusing to paint because they require a separate stencil for each color. Designs with this degree of sophistication read better when they're large. If your home can't carry off patterns of grandiose dimensions, it's best to stick with simple, stylized patterns executed in two or three colors plus a neutral—at least until you become extremely proficient at this craft. But if you can be patient, you can let your stenciled surface become more intricate over time, as you go back over the course of months and build up your pattern. Even professional artists work for weeks, sometimes in teams, to create the subtleties of a multilayered, sophisticated design. As a beginner, allow yourself the time to let your stenciled motif develop slowly.

The basis for successful stenciling lies in the pattern. Study various designs, and you'll notice that often the best examples are simple and stylized. Keeping that in mind, select a motif that complements your room's character and décor. You have many options for finding one. Arts-and-crafts supply stores sell a great variety of precut stencils. They also carry stencil pattern books, which have numerous designs from which to choose. If you find one you like, just trace it. You also can draw your own motif. Look for effective design ideas everywhere—art books, decorating magazines, display houses, fabrics, your carpet, and so on.

You don't have to be an artist to make a stencil. Simply transfer the design onto tracing paper, lay it over a sheet of acetate, which you can buy in an arts-and-crafts supply store, and then cut out the design using a craft knife as instructed under "Making a Stencil," on page 210. If the pattern is too small or too large to use as is, enlarge or reduce it to the correct size on a photocopier, and then transfer it to the acetate.

Note that all stencil patterns link their smaller design elements with narrow strips or "bridges" of the stencil material. These bridges hold the design together, giving it rhythm and continuity. If it's a floral stencil, the bridge might be the stem, for example. If you use a precut stencil or trace from a stencil book, these bridges are the correct width. However, if you copy a pattern from another source or make you own design from scratch, be careful not to make these crucial bridges too thin. They break easily under pressure from the stroke of the stencil brush.

As you develop your pattern, also develop a color scheme. It helps to sketch out the colors you plan to use with colored pencils or markers. This reproduces color pattern as well as the shapes.

Stenciling

- Making a Stencil

- How to Stencil

*A **stenciled vine** wraps around the panels in this garden-inspired dining area.*

Making a Stencil

Decorative painters use a variety of materials to create stencils. The list includes thin posterboard, shellacked stencil paper, and stencil acetate. Acetate is probably the easiest material for a beginner to use.

Once you have your design refined in terms of size, pattern, and color scheme, draw a straight line along its top and bottom edges. Cut or notch small registration marks along the end of these lines. These marks, if made in the same spot, will allow you to align a pattern with a chalk line you'll make on the wall to keep your design straight as you move across the surface. You can also rely on registration marks to line up one pattern on top of another. Trim the paper so that you have about a 1-inch border around the pattern. Run off copies of the pattern on a photocopier, one for each color plus a few extra. If the project calls for three colors, cut three pieces of acetate to the same size as the pattern, and draw a pencil line 1 inch from the bottom or top edges of each sheet, to act as guidelines for placing the paper pattern.

Using masking tape, secure one piece of the stencil acetate to a cutting board. Spray the back of one pattern piece with artist's adhesive, and aligning the pencil lines on the acetate (you can see them through the registration marks) with the lines on the pattern, press the pattern

This stencil design requires a separate cut-out pattern for each of the elements in the design. Notice the registration marks at the end of each of the pattern parts. The numerals I, II, and III that appear in the top corner indicate the colors to use. The large holes in the bottom corner are for tacking the stencils on a wall or board while the paint dries.

piece onto the stencil acetate. Identify all the pattern elements that receive the first color, and cut them out of both paper and acetate using a craft knife. Also cut out the registration marks in the acetate. Label the stencil "#1," mark the top and right sides accordingly, and write the color name on the front. Repeat these steps to make a stencil for each color or element in the pattern.

If you use stencil paper, strengthen the pieces with shellac, which also makes them easy to clean so you can reuse them. Use a disposable roller to apply two coats of shellac to each side of each stencil.

You can use a chalk-line box to make guidelines and a stencil brush to apply the paint.

STENCIL CUTTING

SKILL LEVEL: Intermediate to advanced

PAIRS OF HANDS NEEDED: 1

TOOLS: Pattern; photocopies of pattern; colored pencils or markers; ruler; #2 pencil; scissors; cutting board (a padded wood board, heavy cardboard, rubber or plastic board, or plate glass); craft knife with disposable blades; plenty of replacement blades; stencil material (stencil paper, thick cardboard, or stencil acetate); masking tape; artist's adhesive spray; shellac to strengthen stencil paper if used; disposable roller

Stenciling

Good stenciling requires accurate alignment of the different elements and careful application of the paints. The standard stenciling stroke is a straight up-and-down pouncing motion with a stencil brush that's barely loaded with paint. Pounce so the color is even across the entire design, or slowly lighten your stroke so the color appears to fade as you move from one area to another. Just be sure you fade the same elements the same way each time.

F O R M U L A

STENCILING

SKILL LEVEL: Advanced beginner to advanced, depending on the design's complexity

RECOMMENDED FOR: All smooth, flat, or rounded surfaces

NOT RECOMMENDED FOR: Any surface with intricate carving or elaborate trim

PAIRS OF HANDS NEEDED: 1 or 2

TOOLS: Yardstick; #1 pencil; chalk-line box and light-colored chalk; level or carpenters' spirit level; stencils; paint buckets; small dishes; masking tape; artist's spray adhesive; stencil brush; old newspapers; clean rags; mineral spirits; gloves

BASE COAT: Latex paint

PAINT: Latex or acrylic paint

TYPICAL WORKING SECTION: 1 or 2 linear feet

CLEAR TOP COAT: An optional matte-finish product

How to Stencil

1 Using a chalk-line box and level, make guidelines on the walls at the place where the bottom of the border or stenciled design will sit.

2 Mix the first paint color; in this example, a medium gray was used for the largest elements in the design. Pour a small amount into a dish. Reseal the can to keep the solvent from evaporating.

3 Spray artist's adhesive onto the back of the first stencil. Align the registration marks with the chalk line, and press the stencil into place on the wall. Further secure the stencil by applying strips of masking tape along the edges.

4 Dip a stencil brush into the paint. Off-load excess paint onto old newspaper so that the brush is almost dry. Then dab the brush over the cut-out areas with the pouncing stroke described in the introduction. Keep your touch firm enough to fill the total area, even at the top. If you begin to run out of paint, lift the brush, dab it into the paint, off-load if necessary, and dab again. Work to keep the amount of glaze even from one element of the stencil pattern to the next. Gently lift up the stencil from the bottom just enough to make sure that you have completed all of the parts that require the first color.

6 Mix the second paint color; a dark gray is shown here. Pour a small amount of the paint into a dish. Reseal the can to keep the solvent from evaporating. Then, working the same way as described in Steps 3 to 5, position the second stencil in place, and pounce on the second color. Continue around the room, stenciling all of the design elements that require the second color. Let the surface dry.

5 Carefully remove the stencil, taking care not to smudge the paint. (Check the back of the stencil from time to time, and clean off any paint.) Respray the stencil's back with adhesive, if necessary. Reposition the stencil over the next section, aligning the registration marks and taping the edges as described in Step 3. Pounce on the paint as in Step 4. Continue this way around the room until everything that will receive the first color has been stenciled. Let the surface dry.

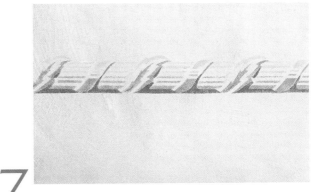

7 Mix the third paint color; a light gray is shown here. Pour a small amount into a dish. Then, working the same way a third time, position and tape the third stencil in place, and pounce on the third color. Continue around the room, stenciling all of the design elements that require this color. Let it dry.

CHAPTER 14

Decorative painting reaches the level of high art with the faux-stone techniques, especially marbling. Applied with glaze and a modicum of patience, they can capture the enduring, earthy beauty of nature for a fraction of the cost of the real thing. Consider these painted elements as economy extravagantly disguised.

Creating Stone Effects

Part of the attraction of these techniques is that they offer an endless array of color and textural combinations with which to work. That's why it pays to spend time studying various types of architectural stone, especially the many varieties of marble, and observe their colors and veining patterns. What you'll eventually create will be impressive and satisfying. Faux-stone finishes may range from realistic renditions to impressionistic interpretations.

Faux-stone techniques were used by artist Lucianna Samu to create a rusticated stone wall and marble columns in this bathroom.

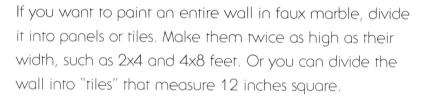

Of course, faux-stone finishes involve some secrets. First, less is more. It's logical to employ these finishes sparingly, as you would the real materials, which are far too expensive to be used lavishly in all but palatial homes, decorated on equally large budgets.

Second, their individual beauty pales when they have to compete with one another or with other painted finishes. For the richest look, limit your faux-stone finishes to one or two per room.

Finally, you create the best effects when you use these finishes on surfaces that logically could be made of natural stone, such as floors, fireplace mantels and surrounds, table tops, countertops, accent walls, vanity tops, tub surrounds, columns, and other architectural accessories.

If you want to paint an entire wall in faux marble, divide it into panels or tiles. Make them twice as high as their width, such as 2x4 and 4x8 feet. Or you can divide the wall into "tiles" that measure 12 inches square.

The Marble Story

Marble is metamorphic rock that, due to thousands of years of heat and pressure and the presence of impurities, has formed in distinctive patterns. There are hundreds of types of marble, each named for the region where it is found, and each distinct in its markings and color. Subtle coloring, fragmented patterns, and complicated veining makes marble the most exacting finish to paint. You have to paint in a way that makes its features meld into one exquisite whole, rather than stand out as individual elements.

A bleached turkey feather and a broad knife
are tools that are commonly used for various faux-stone techniques.

First, concern yourself with creating the drifts of color. In nature these drifts are the result of molten minerals diffusing within the stone at some point during its formation. They have a blurred appearance and flow in one direction. Capture that look by running glaze at an angle in elongated lines that merge and diverge as they travel across the surface. Avoid making the ends of the shapes into sharply pointed triangles—keep them irregular. Vary the lines in width, as shown in the techniques presented in this chapter.

Sharper, more distinct veins intermix with these drifts of color. Think of them as cracks traveling through the marble at the same angle. Using the edge of a bleached turkey feather, paint the veins as fine but meandering, uneven lines of varying widths. Make your veins realistic by keeping these features in mind as you lay them down:

- Veins don't run at exact right angles to one another.
- Veins don't run perfectly parallel to one another.
- Veins don't branch off at the end like forks in a road.
- Veins don't come to a sudden end. Rather, they move out to and off the edge of the surface.
- Veins don't crisscross like an X.
- Veins don't end in sharp points like triangles.
- Veins don't line up in regular, repetitive patterns.
- Veins don't zigzag or form wiggly lines.

Many of the faux-stone finishes call for the use of negative techniques introduced in Chapter 7, "Ragging," beginning on page 140. Take time to review the application methods, particularly ones involving cheeseclothing and newspaper blending, before you begin any stone finish.

Creating Stone Effects

- White Marble

- Jasper

- Serpentine Marble

- A Rusticated Stone Wall

- Slate

- A Stone Inset

White Marble

This decorative finish captures the pristine beauty of an expensive stone. Actually, it's one of the easiest to depict in paint because it's a breccia marble—one that's broken into many small, irregular color fragments separated by black veins. Study real white marble, and you'll notice that the colors flow or drift in one dominant direction. Plan the direction of your faux marble's drift and how the black veins will fragment before you start painting. Sketch your veining plan on a piece of paper with the same proportions as the area you'll be painting. Also plan the layout of the panels if you're painting a large surface. The drift and veins on adjoining panels should mirror one another—in walls made from real marble, adjacent slabs of rock are installed next to one another, with one of the pieces flopped to create a mirror-image effect.

Don't forget to base-coat your surface with a cool-white latex paint, and let it dry thoroughly before you proceed.

How to Create White Marble

1   Mix the white and black glazes to the desired thickness. Pour a small amount of each glaze into the paint trays. Seal the cans to keep the solvent from evaporating.

2   Brush or roll the white glaze onto the surface. Use a roller on a large area such as a wall panel.

3   Working quickly, lay the black glaze drift lines onto the white glaze using a decorator brush with the bristles laid on the surface at about a 45-degree angle. Leave some of the drift lines solid, and smudge others into the wet white glaze so that they begin to turn gray, as shown.

4 *Texture the drift lines, and lift off excess glaze by pressing sheets of newspaper over the entire surface, as shown. This pulls the colors over one another. Work diagonally across the surface, and change the angle of the sheets frequently to avoid producing a recognizable pattern. When a sheet becomes gooey, discard it and use a new one.*

5 *Hold a clean decorator brush at an angle, as shown, and pounce it along the seams between the white paint and the black glaze. Blend the black glaze into the white glaze so that just a little of the pure white glaze remains, but don't lose all the texture.*

6 *Depending on your dominant hand, take a right-hand or left-hand bleached turkey feather, and dip it into the black glaze. Barely touching its edge to the surface, tickle in vein lines that converge and diverge with the mineralized areas. These lines should tremble slightly but not zigzag or squiggle. The goal is to make the finer veins look as if they originated deep inside the marble, not on its surface.*

7 *Make an overglaze with white paint. Brush it onto the entire surface, and then blot it by pressing newspapers over the surface as described in Step 4. This sinks the colors into one another and helps create the depth and translucence that is characteristic of marble.*

8 *The final finish: The timeless beauty of white marble created in paint. The look is subtle, yet complex and intriguing.*

FORMULA

WHITE MARBLE

SKILL LEVEL: Advanced intermediate to advanced

RECOMMENDED FOR: Any surface that could be covered with real marble; large walls and floors, if divided into panels

NOT RECOMMENDED FOR: Large surfaces such as walls, unless divided into panels; surfaces with intricate carving or elaborate trim

PAIRS OF HANDS NEEDED: 1

TOOLS: Paint buckets; mixing sticks; roller with low-nap cover or foam; 2 paint trays; 2 3-inch-wide decorator brushes; old newspapers; bleached turkey feather; mineral spirits; gloves

BASE COAT: White flat alkyd paint

GLAZE COLORANTS: Custom-mixed white and black flat, eggshell, or satin alkyd paints, or universal tints

GLAZE FORMULA: 1 part colorant, 1 part alkyd glazing medium, and 1 part mineral spirits

OVERGLAZE FORMULA: 1 part white satin alkyd paint to 1 to 4 parts solvent

TYPICAL WORKABLE AREA: A 4x8-foot area

CLEAR TOP COAT: Yes. Use a nonyellowing product

Jasper

Mentioned in the Bible, jasper is considered a precious stone even though it's a form of quartz. Jasper comes in a variety of colors—yellow, brown, green, and red—that give it its exotic quality. Although jasper is often associated with green, red jasper (which gets some of its color from iron ore) makes a handsome wall because its texture is quite graphic and masculine. As a faux stone, it lends itself easily to creating a paneled-wall effect. Plus, it's as handsome as marble and much faster and easier to create.

Start with an under-scumble: random coats of full-bodied latex paint slapped over a base coat of warm-white flat latex paint that's thoroughly dry. Then apply different colors of oil glazes, texturing them with newspaper and bunched cheesecloth. Review instruction's for both techniques before you begin by consulting Chapter 7, "Ragging," starting on page 140.

How to Create Jasper

1 *Cut one cheesecloth into 6-foot-long pieces, and set the pieces aside. Mix the gray and rust oil glazes to the desired color and thickness. Seal the cans to keep the solvent from evaporating, and set them aside until needed.*

2 *To make the under-scumble, brush or roll intense yellow full-bodied latex paint onto the surface using random strokes. Make the strokes on a diagonal, as shown. Cover about 70 percent of the surface, leaving much of the white base coat showing. Use a roller on a large surface.*

3 Working the same way and in the same direction as in Step 2, slap on full-bodied orange latex paint using random strokes. Cover some of the yellow paint and some of the base coat so that 80 percent of the surface is hidden. That leaves about 20 percent of the white base color showing through.

4 Continuing on a diagonal, brush the gray glaze over the yellow strokes and the rust glaze over the orange strokes. Blend the glazes, and pull them over the white base coat as you brush.

5 Press newspaper over the glazed surface to further blend the colors and lift off the excess, as described in "Creating a Parchment Effect with Newsprint," page 158. If it takes up too much glaze, apply some gray glaze to the newspaper, and press it in place to redeposit glaze onto the surface.

6 Pat cheesecloth over the surface with up-and-down strokes, to fold in the texture and continue to blend the colors. Turn the cloth frequently so that you don't create an identifiable pattern.

7 *If desired, make an overglaze by thinning the rust glaze with solvent; brush it over the dry surface. Immediately pick up the excess glaze by texturing with newspaper as described in Step 5. Follow up by texturing with a bunched cheesecloth, as described in Step 6. Repeat until the entire surface is covered. This overglaze process further blends and softens the finish.*

8 *The final finish. Using the optional overglaze means you don't have to work as hard on the first steps in the process. Either way, the result is subtle yet exotic color variations that create a handsome stone look. After the glazing dries, use a low-luster varnish if you want a clear top coat.*

F O R M U L A

JASPER

SKILL LEVEL: Advanced intermediate to advanced

RECOMMENDED FOR: Small surfaces or large walls and floors, if divided into panels

NOT RECOMMENDED FOR: Any surface with intricate carving or elaborate trim

PAIRS OF HANDS NEEDED: 1

TOOLS: Painter's masking tape; paint buckets; mixing sticks; 2 paint trays; several rollers with low-nap or foam covers; several 3-inch-wide decorator brushes; old newspapers; 6-foot-long pieces of 90-weight cheesecloth; clean rags; mineral spirits; gloves

BASE COAT: Warm-white satin latex paint

UNDER SCUMBLE: Custom-mixed flat alkyd paints or universal tints

GLAZE COLORANTS: Custom-mixed alkyd paints

GLAZE FORMULA: 1 part colorant, 1 part alkyd glazing medium, and 1 part mineral spirits

OVERGLAZE: 1 part colorant, 1 part alkyd glazing liquid, and 8 parts mineral spirits

TYPICAL WORKABLE SECTION: A 4x8-foot area

CLEAR TOP COAT: Optional

Serpentine Marble

Known in Italy as *verde antico* and in France as *verd antique*, this dramatic green marble has strong white veins and an emphatic texture created by alternating dark and light areas. It's quite easy to create with oil glazes. An experienced faux painter can execute it in latex paint, but a beginner should stick with an oil glaze because it will allow more time to work the wet surface.

The project begins by applying a deep-green base coat of latex or alkyd paint and then allowing it to thoroughly dry. It continues with the application of three oil glazes—white, deep green, and black—and texturing with newspaper and bunched cheesecloth. Feather veining with white glaze follows. Finally, the entire surface is softened with an overglaze. Although the process involves numerous steps, it's easy to complete.

How to Create Serpentine Marble

1 Cut cheesecloth into 6-foot-long pieces, and set the pieces aside. Mix the white, green, and black oil glazes to the desired colors and thicknesses. The green glaze should be a deeper version of the base-coat color. Pour a small amount of the white glaze into the paint tray. Seal all of the cans to keep the solvent from evaporating.

2 Working on a diagonal, slap on the white glaze as shown. Use random, curving strokes that cover 50 percent of the surface.

3 Working as in Step 2, pour a small amount of green glaze into a paint tray, and slap it on. Cover about 50 percent of the surface, with some of the green overlapping the white. The surface should be completely covered with white and green glaze.

4 Working the same way again, slap on the black glaze, as shown. Cover about 25 percent of the surface, overlapping both white and green strokes. This further blends the colors.

5 Blend the colors some more, and texture the glazes by pressing sheets of newspaper over the surface. Work on a diagonal and continually turn the sheets in different directions to avoid producing a recognizable pattern.

6 Bunch a piece of cheesecloth in your hand so that it forms soft folds. Pat it over the surface to do some final blending of the three colors, and make the texture even and more regular.

7 At this point, the marble is a mix of shifting dark and light areas, lit from within by glimpses of white and medium green. It's now ready for you to apply its veins.

8 Dip a bleached turkey feather into the white glaze, and tickle on the veins, following the instructions in the introduction, pages 216–217, and in "White Marble," pages 218–220. Remember: When painting veins, less is more.

9 Make an overglaze by thinning the deep green glaze so that it's 50 to 80 percent mineral spirits. Brush the overglaze over the entire surface. Pat the glaze with a piece of bunched cheesecloth to soften it and sink the veins into the surface.

10 The final finish: an elegant faux-marble finish, featuring a subtle blend of dramatic colors and intermingled veins.

Masterstroke

To give faux marble an authentic fossilized appearance, try this: Before the glaze dries, dip an old, soft toothbrush into mineral spirits, and hold it over the painted surface. Then drag your thumb down across the bristles toward you. This action will lightly spray the surface with a minute amount of solvent, just enough to slightly repel some of the paint and reveal a little of the underlying surface in spots.

FORMULA

SERPENTINE MARBLE

SKILL LEVEL: Advanced intermediate to advanced

RECOMMENDED FOR: Any small or large surface that could be real stone; columns or floors

NOT RECOMMENDED FOR: Any surface with intricate carving or elaborate trim

PAIRS OF HANDS NEEDED: 1

TOOLS: Painter's masking tape; paint buckets; mixing sticks; 3 paint trays; 3 3-inch-wide decorator brushes; old newspapers; 6-foot-long pieces of 90-weight cheesecloth; bleached turkey feathers; clean rags; mineral spirits; gloves

BASE COAT: Green custom-mixed latex paint

GLAZE COLORANTS: Custom-mixed flat, eggshell, or satin alkyd paints

GLAZE FORMULA: 1 part colorant, 1 part alkyd glazing medium, and 1 part mineral spirits

OVERGLAZE FORMULA: 1 part colorant, 1 part alkyd glazing medium, and 2 to 8 parts mineral spirits

TYPICAL WORKING AREA: A 4x8-foot area

CLEAR TOP COAT: Yes

A Rusticated Stone Wall

This faux finish creates the look of mortared stone blocks. It's another classic device, one that has been used for centuries. (George Washington hired painters to create Mount Vernon's rusticated stonelike exterior with one version of the technique.) It's also the easiest faux finish to render, next to basic sponging, and an excellent project for a beginner because work is done in small, controlled sections.

Carrying out a rusticated stone finish is only slightly laborious in the beginning. You have to measure and draw the lines for the blocks, and press masking tape in place between the spaces. However, the tedious part of the job ends there. Once you have defined your blocks, you can divide your work into a number of small, easily managed areas, which makes it easier. Plus, glazing individual blocks allows you to stop and start work whenever and wherever you wish (except in the middle of a block). In addition, more than one person can paint the blocks at the same time. The variations in tone produced by different hands enhances the natural look of individual "stones."

For an authentic-looking imitation of stone, try to vary the tones of the paint's color by applying different amounts of pressure.

Making the Blocks

First, decide on the size of your blocks. A standard rectangular stone block is twice as long as it is high, but sizes can vary to suit your space. Take time to do some research on block work. If you can't find a helpful book in the library, talk to a local stone distributor. Stone blocks have two measurements: *nominal* size and the smaller *actual* size, which allows for the thickness of the mortar between the blocks. Use the nominal size when drawing the blocks on the surface you will paint. Once you've determined the block size, plan the total layout on graph paper. This is important if you want to cover a large area, even if it's only a dado on the bottom third of a wall. When sketching your plan, remember: Stagger the courses of blocks so that the end of one course aligns with the center of the one immediately above and below it.

Make your blocks level with the ceiling as opposed to the floor.

Paint the wall with a base coat of warm-white flat latex paint, and allow it to dry thoroughly; then draw the grid. Using your layout as a guide, go to one corner of the wall, and measure down from the ceiling to the point where the first two courses of block will meet. Lightly mark this point with a pencil. Do the same in the opposite corner. Using a chalk-line box or spirit level, snap a guideline between the two marks, and lightly pencil in this horizontal line along the entire length of the wall. Because most walls are not truly level, you'll have to make the blocks appear level with the ceiling, not the floor; any deviation, no matter how slight, will be more obvious at the ceiling line than the floor line.

Using this first line as a reference, measure for and lightly pencil in the remaining horizontal lines, and then mark the vertical lines for each block. Center pieces of painter's masking tape over each horizontal line, and press it into place. Press pieces of the same tape into place over the center of each vertical line. Use a razor blade or utility knife to cut the vertical tapes, making them even with the outside edges of the horizontal ones. With the grid established, paint the blocks with full-bodied flat latex paint custom-mixed to the desired stone hue. Here, the same warm-white paint used to base coat the wall is altered slightly with taupe and beige to make a realistic stone color.

How to Paint a Rusticated Stone Wall

1 With the grid for the blocks marked (with pencil or chalk lines) apply painter's masking tape to create the mortar lines. Press the painter's masking tape over the center of each line as described in "Making the Blocks," page 229. Vertical lines should be staggered in adjacent courses and centered on the block above, as shown.

2 Mix full-bodied flat latex paint to the desired stone color, pour a small amount into the paint tray. Seal the can, and set it aside to prevent spillage.

3 Using a decorator brush, apply the paint. Pounce and twist the brush to create a stonelike texture. Vary the coloration from block to block by applying different amounts of pressure with the brush.

4 Allow the blocks to dry completely. Pull off the tape by lifting the ends and pulling them toward you. You might be pleased with this look just as it is; it can be elegant, particularly if you used 1/4-inch-wide tape to mark the grout lines. However, for a more realistic representation, especially on exterior walls and on interior walls that receive a lot of natural light, you should create shadow lines, which are described in Step 5.

5 *Determine the sun's orientation: Shadow lines fall along the right side and the bottom, or the left side and the bottom of the stones. Take the darkest color mixed into the stone paint, and thin it with water. With a broad knife as your guide, paint the shadow lines around two sides of each stone using an artist's brush. When these lines are dry, thin full-bodied white paint, and paint the mortar lines around the blocks. Leave the shadow lines untouched except for clipping their bottom corners.*

6 *The final stone wall: a handsome traditional surface complete with highlights and shadows. Note how the mottled surface of the blocks varies from one to another.*

FORMULA

A RUSTICATED STONE WALL

SKILL LEVEL: Advanced beginner to intermediate

RECOMMENDED FOR: Any flat wall

NOT RECOMMENDED FOR: Any wall with intricate carving or elaborate molding, ceilings, floors, or trim

PAIRS OF HANDS NEEDED: 1 or 2, depending on the size of the wall

TOOLS: ¼- or ½-inch-scale graph paper; #1 pencil; retractable measuring tape; spirit level or chalk line; metal yardstick; ¼-inch-wide painter's masking tape; scissors; razor blade or utility knife; paint bucket; mixing sticks; paint tray; 3-inch-wide decorator brush; 8- to 12-inch-wide broad knife; 2 #6 artist's brushes; clean rags; bucket of clean water; gloves

BASE COAT: Warm-white latex paint

PAINT COLORANT: Warm-white flat latex paint tinted to stone color with taupe and beige universal tints or artist's acrylics

TYPICAL WORKABLE SECTION: One block at a time

CLEAR TOP COAT: No

A real slate sample is an excellent model for your rendering in paint.

Slate

It takes real commitment to make a faux-slate surface, because once you've painted it, it's there for good—at least, it would be a lot of trouble to remove. Admittedly, this is a handsome finish for walls, ceilings, and furniture (such as table tops), so don't be deterred if you truly want to create this look and texture.

Beyond this decision, executing the technique is easy. You simply trowel textured latex paint onto a surface right out of the can. Use a white textured paint, or purchase custom-mixed paint in a slate gray as featured in this example. You can achieve the same look by painting on regular drywall compound, but unlike textured paint, it isn't self-sealing. That means you must sand and prime it before base-coating—a difficult prospect on the uneven surface you're creating here. Using the textured paint makes sense because it's much easier and requires fewer steps.

Buy a medium-smooth textured latex paint, and have it custom-mixed to the desired base color; here, it's a medium gray. Prime or base-coat the surface, as desired. When the base coat is thoroughly dry, proceed with creating this handsome finish.

How to Create a Slate Surface

1 Cut cheesecloth into 6-foot-long pieces, and set them aside. Mix the glaze to the desired color and thickness. Seal the can, and set it aside.

2 Using a broad knife, spread the textured paint onto the surface at a 45-degree angle. Cover about 75 percent of the surface. Don't worry about leaving voids in the surface; they help create the desired texture.

3 Base-coat the textured paint with a slightly deeper color than the textured paint color. Brush or roll this coat on, as desired. Again, ignore voids, but cover most of the surface.

4 Pour a small amount of the glaze into the paint tray. Reseal the can to keep the solvent from evaporating. Brush or roll the glaze over 100 percent of a workable area (about 30 square feet). Don't worry about brush marks; they will flatten out as the glaze begins to mat down. It should eventually look like this.

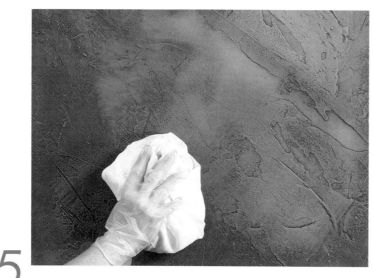

5 *Immediately take a bunched cheesecloth dampened with mineral spirits, and lightly dab it over the surface with straight up-and-down strokes. Then rub the cloth over the high points to take off the glaze and mottle the surface, but don't let it absorb glaze from the recessed areas. If too much paint comes off in spots, apply more and rework the area.*

6 *The slate finish. It has the flinty, layered texture characteristic of real slate, as well as the durability. Faux slate also can be rendered in brown and black-green. If you want a deeper gray than shown in this example, simply use a darker base coat.*

FORMULA

SLATE

SKILL LEVEL: Advanced beginner to intermediate

RECOMMENDED FOR: Walls, ceilings, and furniture

NOT RECOMMENDED FOR: Floors, countertops, or any surface with intricate carving or elaborate trim

PAIRS OF HANDS NEEDED: 1

TOOLS: Paint buckets; 8-inch-wide broad knife; paint tray; 3-inch-wide decorator brush; roller with low-nap or foam cover; 6-foot-long pieces of 90-weight cheesecloth; clean rags; mineral spirits; gloves

BASE COAT: Custom-mixed latex paint

TEXTURE COAT: Custom-mixed flat latex textured paint, medium smooth

GLAZE COLORANT: Custom-mixed alkyd paint or universal tints

GLAZE FORMULA: 1 part colorant, 1 part alkyd glazing medium, and 2 to 3 parts mineral spirits

TYPICAL WORKABLE SECTION: A 30-square-foot area

CLEAR TOP COAT: No

A Stone Inset

It's possible to achieve the look of inset stone on a floor with paint. It takes an accurate scale drawing, a thoughtful color scheme, careful measurements, a lot of masking and painting, and several helpers, but the result is worth the effort. You'll have as handsome a floor as one tiled with expensive natural materials such as marble, granite, or ceramic tile.

Although the prospect of painting an entire floor may seem daunting, this technique, like the rusticated stone wall technique (page 228), lets you stop and start wherever you want to, which means you can work over as long a period of time as you wish.

Start by developing your design on graph paper. Let each square represent an exact measurement so it transfers to the floor with ease. Most floors don't form perfect squares or rectangles, so begin the layout in the exact center of the floor, and work out toward the edges.

Next, develop the complete color scheme on graph paper. Make samples of each color to accurately test their overall effect. (See "Mixing Paints and Glazes," Chapter 5, beginning on page 106.) Before painting,

How to Paint an Inset Field

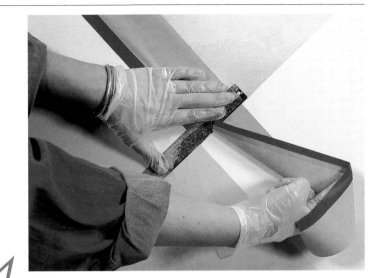

1 Plan to paint two adjoining squares of the same color at one time. Mask each square by taping just outside its line on one side with wide paper tape and painter's masking tape, as shown. Using a straightedge as a guide, tear the tape at the corner. Tape the opposite side the same way.

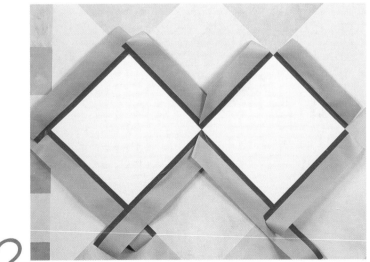

2 Tape the other two sides of each square the same way, but tear the inner corners where the two squares meet at an angle, as shown.

clean the floor thoroughly, even stripping it with a sander if necessary. Then paint the floor with one coat of exterior-grade latex primer, followed by two coats of exterior-grade white semigloss latex enamel. Let each of these layers cure thoroughly before applying the next one.

Using a straightedge, a retractable metal measuring tape, and a chalk-line box, mark the design's grid on the floor. Trace over the chalk lines with a pencil. Then rub the chalk lines off with a damp sponge. To create a border around your design, as shown in Step 6, press painter's masking tape in place just outside the border's inner edge. Then choose one color to paint first. Place masking tape just outside the vertical lines defining the blocks for that color, and press it in place. Paint the first sections the desired color, and let them dry thoroughly. Remove the masking tape. Repeat the process to tape and paint the remaining sections with the second color.

Let the border dry completely; then remove the masking tape by lifting the end and pulling toward you. Cover the border areas with plastic sheeting to protect them. You're now ready to paint the floor's field design.

3 Make sure the two taped squares come together at a 90-degree angle, and that the taped seals are tight.

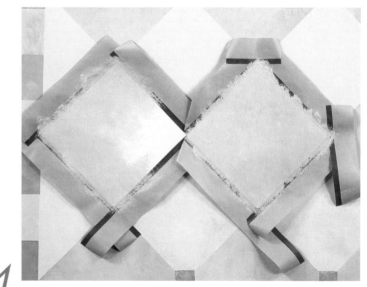

4 Pounce the paint over the squares to color them and give them some texture. Let them dry thoroughly before painting the next two squares. Repeat the two-squares-at-a-time method until all the large squares are covered. Let the surface dry thoroughly. Remove all the tape by lifting the end of each piece and pulling it toward you.

5 Using the same measuring and taping technique, mask all the insets on the floor. Paint them the desired color, and let them dry thoroughly. Then remove all the tape as instructed in Step 4.

6 The final effect. Elegant with its geometric pattern and soft colors, all this floor needs is a protective layer of satin polyurethane to keep it handsome over time.

F O R M U L A

A STONE INSET

SKILL LEVEL: Advanced

RECOMMENDED FOR: Floors and paneling for flat walls

NOT RECOMMENDED FOR: Ceilings and any surface with intricate carving or elaborate trim

PAIRS OF HANDS NEEDED: 2 or 3

TOOLS: ¼-inch or ½-inch graph paper; #1 pencil; colored pencils; sample boards; paint buckets; mixing sticks; paint tray; roller with low-nap cover; retractable metal measuring tape; straightedge; chalk line; sponge; bucket of clean water; paper tape; painter's masking tape; 1½- and 2½-inch-wide decorator brushes; bucket of clean water; clean rags; gloves

PRIMER: Latex primer

BASE COAT: Exterior-grade white latex paint

STONE PAINTS: Custom-mixed flat latex paint

TYPICAL WORKABLE SECTION: 2 stones at a time

CLEAR TOP COAT: Satin-finish polyurethane

Like the faux-stone finishes, wood graining is a high art based on centuries of tradition. Ancient cultures, such as the Chinese, Egyptians, and Romans, used it to create the illusion of something they admired but had very little of—wood. Called *faux bois* in Europe, these techniques never lost popularity there for much the same reason. They are becoming more popular here in America, as once-plentiful supplies of wood dwindle and finish-grade wood becomes more expensive. Even if it was affordable, concern for saving the forests focuses attention on wood graining as an ecologically sound alternative.

Wood Graining

As with marbling, creating realistic wood grains with paint is an exacting technique that demands accurate rendering. It takes years to master, but you can begin with some basics.

Pleasing wood-grain finishes *can be accomplished by employing some basic methods. The complex designs on display in this bathroom, however, require masterful skills.*

Understanding Wood

These graining methods require at least a rudimentary understanding of wood. Take some time to study the subject before you attempt any of the techniques.

You'll discover each wood species has its own grain pattern and color. However, that grain pattern depends on more than the tree's species. The specific tree's growth pattern, the part of the tree from which the wood was taken, and how the tree was cut into boards all influence it. As you study wood, focus on the two most common grain patterns: straight grain and heart grain.

Straight grain results from cutting a tree into quarters lengthwise. Each quarter in turn is cut into wedges, and then the wedges into boards. This is quarter-sawn wood; the grain runs straight down the board and appears as straight lines of varying widths and colors on the end of the board. The tree's annual growth rings make this pattern.

Heart grain results from cutting through the tree with parallel vertical cuts running across the tree's full width. This type of grain goes by many names, among them cathedral grain, V-grain, plain sawn, and flat sawn. They all describe the same thing, a V-shaped grain pattern made by the tree's annual growth rings. This pattern is often described as flame-shaped. Pay careful attention to these grain patterns. Take time to study natural wood, both raw and finished, to see how these patterns work. This is important if you plan to render the heart grain by hand with a brush. Although these grain lines run parallel to one

Three specialty brushes *that are commonly used for wood graining include (clockwise from top left) the six-part pipe grainer, a flogging brush (also called a dragger), and a 12-part pipe grainer.*

another, they are separated by uneven spaces. They vary in width, have uneven jogs along the edges, and end slightly rounded, not in sharp points. Finally, they always reach to the edges of a specific section; they don't stop in the middle of it.

Tools such as graining heels and graining rockers make faux techniques much easier, but they require an unusual motion. You must rock them in small increments while you pull the stroke across the surface. Take time to practice this movement before you apply it to a painted surface.

Most wood grains are done in workable-sized planks and panels. Render them using base coats and glazes that are close in tone, with the base coat always lighter than the glaze. For the most part, you can achieve these finishes with oil-based glazes and apply a clear top coat of satin oil varnish.

The basic wood-graining glaze consists of 1 part universal tints, 1 part boiled linseed oil, 2 parts satin oil varnish, and 3 parts mineral spirits. Mix the linseed oil, oil varnish, and mineral spirits; then add the universal tints until you have the wood tone you want. Use the earth-tone universal tints—raw umber, burnt umber, raw sienna, burnt sienna, and yellow ochre.

This all-purpose formula works well in most situations. However, problems sometimes occur. If the glaze goes on too slow, you've used too much linseed oil. If it seems too slick, you've added too much varnish to the mix. If it's runny, it contains too much thinner. If the universal tints don't blend thoroughly into the mixture, you've used too much colorant. The solution is to rework the proportions to get a usable mixture.

Wood Graining

- Straight-Grain Mahogany

- Heart-Grain Mahogany

- Knotty Pine

- Oak

- A Burled Panel

Straight-Grain Mahogany

This handsome, reddish wood comes from tropical trees and is highly favored for making cabinets and paneling. It has a fine, straight grain with alternating light and dark tones that add considerably to its appeal. Its faux version is relatively easy to render with paint and wood-graining glaze precisely because its grain is so straight.

Start by base-coating the surface with eggshell or satin latex or alkyd enamel paint that's been custom-mixed to a color that matches the lightest tone in the wood. Let this base coat become thoroughly dry before proceeding. As you move from one step to another, you'll have to switch brushes and change the position for handling them, so pay close attention to the instructions and refer to the accompanying photos.

Keep a supply of clean cloths handy; when a cloth becomes loaded with glaze, discard it for a new one. Don't use any cloth that has frayed edges; small threads can get into the glaze and mar the finish.

How to Create Straight-Grain Mahogany

1 *Cut cheesecloth or other soft, lint-free cotton material into several 6-foot-long pieces. Fold the pieces into pads, and set them aside. Mix the glaze to the desired color and thickness. Pour a small amount into a paint tray. Seal the can to keep the solvent from evaporating.*

2 *Brush or roll the glaze onto the surface. Take a cloth pad, and hold it with your thumb under it and your fingers spread apart on top of it. Pull the pad through the glaze, from the top to the bottom in straight, parallel strokes. The glaze lifts away wherever your fingers touch it.*

3 *Holding a flogging brush by the handle, set it as parallel to the surface as possible. Starting at the top and working straight down, softly slap the brush against the glaze. This establishes a sub-texture and takes the glaze to a workable consistency. Clean the brush frequently.*

4 *Keeping a clean varnish brush as parallel to the surface as possible, firmly press it against the surface. Drag it straight down the glazed surface with a slight squiggling or trembling movement. This further sets up the grain's texture.*

5 *Hold another varnish brush at a 45-degree angle to the surface, and pull it through the glaze with firm vertical strokes to create highlights. Make these strokes in random strips running from the top to the bottom. Flog over the highlight strokes. (See Step 3.)*

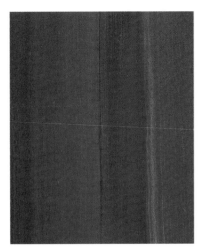

6 *Finished straight-grain mahogany. It produces a handsome surface with great depth of color. Seal with a clear top coat of satin oil varnish.*

FORMULA

STRAIGHT-GRAIN MAHOGANY

SKILL LEVEL: Advanced

RECOMMENDED FOR: Wall panels; floors; millwork such as doors, moldings, and paneling; cabinetry; furniture; and accessories

NOT RECOMMENDED FOR: Walls, except when divided into panels, or any surface with intricate carving or elaborate trim

PAIRS OF HANDS NEEDED: 1

TOOLS: Paint buckets; mixing sticks; paint tray; roller with low-nap or foam cover; pads of 90-weight cheesecloth or other soft, lint-free cotton cut into 6-foot-long pieces; 3-inch-wide flogging brush; 2 3-inch-wide varnish brushes; clean rags; mineral spirits; gloves

BASE COAT: Custom-mixed eggshell or satin latex or alkyd enamel

GLAZE COLORANT: Universal tints

GLAZE FORMULA: 1 part universal tints, 1 part boiled linseed oil, 2 parts satin oil varnish, and 3 parts mineral spirits

TYPICAL WORKABLE SECTION: 2 10- to 12-inch-wide planks

CLEAR TOP COAT: Satin oil varnish

Heart-Grain Mahogany

Its gently arched flame makes heart-grain mahogany a favorite for paneling, doors, and cabinets—any surface where the pattern shows to advantage.

Many of the steps in this technique are the same as those in "Straight-Grain Mahogany," pages 242–243. Review them before you proceed. As with straight-grained mahogany, start by base-coating the surface with an eggshell or satin latex or alkyd enamel, custom-mixed to a color that matches the lightest color in the wood you're mimicking. Let that base coat become thoroughly dry before you proceed.

Masterstroke

A wood-graining technique looks great when applied to an old painted paneled door. Start with the horizontal rails—first paint the top one, then the middle (if there is one), and finally the bottom rail. For the vertical members (stiles), drag the brush starting at the top outside corners, and work your way inside to where they intersect with the horizontal rails.

How to Create Heart-Grain Mahogany

1   Prepare the cloth pads and glaze as described in Step 1 in "Straight-Grain Mahogany," page 242.

2   Brush or roll the glaze onto the surface. Take a cloth pad, and hold it with your thumb under it and your fingers spread apart on top of it. Slightly curve the pad, as shown, as you gently pull it through the glaze. At this point the glaze should still be very workable.

3 Flog the glaze. Hold a flogging brush by the handle, and set it parallel with the surface; then softly slap the glazed surface with the brush. Begin at the top, and work down. This creates a subtexture that makes the glaze more workable. Clean the brush frequently during this step.

4 Wait until the glaze begins to reach snap time; it no longer looks wet at this point. Mask off the plank's heart-grain section. Using a pipe grainer or a used decorator brush that has been notched, lay new glaze on top of the first glaze in the heart-grain pattern. Use a light touch, and don't move the under-glaze in the process. Basically, this step reactivates the glaze; the drier it is, the better the reactivation.

5 Brush out the heart grain by pulling a clean, dry decorator brush through it. This softens and diffuses it into the background grain. Work from the bottom up.

6 Flog the entire plank a second time to create more texture, using the technique described in Step 3, "Straight-Grain Mahogany," page 242.

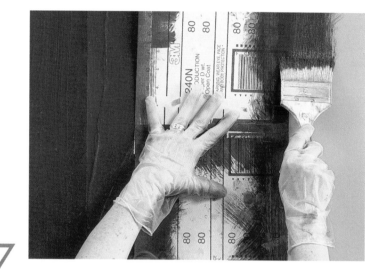

7 *Lay sandpaper, grit-side down, along the "plank's" edges, as shown, to make a straightedge. Apply glaze to the next plank, and repeat the previous steps. Continue in this manner until the entire surface is wood-grained. The glaze along the edges of the sandpaper creates the illusion of separate planks joined together.*

8 *The heart-grain mahogany finish. The flame-shaped grain makes a dramatic texture when used to create faux paneling on a surface. Finish with a top coat of satin oil varnish.*

FORMULA

HEART-GRAIN MAHOGANY

SKILL LEVEL: Advanced

RECOMMENDED FOR: Paneled walls; floors; millwork such as flat doors, plain moldings, and paneling; cabinetry; furniture; and accessories

NOT RECOMMENDED FOR: Walls, except when divided into panels, or any surface with intricate craving or elaborate trim

PAIRS OF HANDS NEEDED: 1

TOOLS: Paint buckets; mixing sticks; roller with low-nap cover or foam cover; pads of 90-weight cheesecloth or other soft cotton cut into 6-foot-long pieces; 3-inch-wide flogging brush; pads of soft, lint-free cotton; pipe grainer or notched decorator brush; sheets of 80-grit sandpaper; clean rags; mineral spirits; gloves

BASE COAT: Custom-mixed eggshell or satin latex or alkyd enamel

GLAZE COLORANT: Universal tints

GLAZE FORMULA: 1 part universal tints, 1 part boiled linseed oil, 2 parts satin oil varnish, and 3 parts mineral spirits

TYPICAL WORKABLE SECTION: 10- to 12-inch-wide plank

CLEAR TOP COAT: Satin oil varnish

Knotty Pine

Its very informality makes this popular wood easy to re-create in paint. In real wood, knots can be found in the cut branches that grow out of the tree trunk. If you study the cuts in pine, you'll notice that there are oval and round knots, ingrown knots and loose knots, as well as knots that run across the entire face of a board. Each type is the result of how the wood has been cut or how the tree grew. And there are other characteristics of knots that can make your rendering more realistic, as well. Some knots look smudgy, for example. Sometimes the straight grain around the knot swirls. Visit a mill or lumberyard to study the patterns of knotty pine before starting your project. When you're ready to begin, base-coat the surface using a warm-white flat latex paint. Let the base coat become thoroughly dry before you proceed.

Because you'll need clean strips of cotton or cheesecloth to create the knots and soften the effects, keep a supply of them handy. When one becomes covered with glaze, discard it for a clean piece. Also, don't use strips of cloth with frayed edges. Loose threads that get into the wet glaze will mar the finished result.

How to Create Knotty Pine

1 *Cut cheesecloth or other soft, lint-free cotton material into 6-foot-long pieces; shape them into loose rolls, and set them aside. Tint the remaining base coat with universal tints to the lightest color in natural pine. Mix a slightly deeper color, and thin it with water to a 50-50 glaze. Also, mix a deeper brown color for painting the knots.*

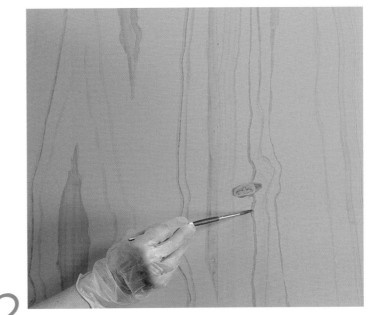

2 *Cover the plank with the lightest color. Create the knots, as shown, using an artist's brush and the deeper color paint. Then paint in the grain lines using the thinned paint and an artist's brush. Make the lines tight around the knot's center and thicker and more elongated as they move outward. Don't over-do the amount of grain or the number of knots you paint. Remember, less is more if you want a realistic result.*

3 *Apply the glaze to the planks using a decorator brush. Then wrap a piece of cotton over your thumb, press it into the center of each knot, and wiggle it around to remove some of the glaze. Create lighter areas along some of the grain lines by wiping along the grain lines with the cloth, as shown.*

4 *Soften the overall effect and establish checks (the cut rays) with a rolled cloth. Push the cloth into the glaze and pull it straight out—away from the surface— to lift off some of the glaze. Keep turning the cloth in your hand so only a clean cloth surface touches the glaze. When a roll becomes saturated with glaze, discard it and use a new one. Repeat this movement over the entire surface. Then flog the surface, following the instructions in Step 3, "Straight-Grain Mahogany," page 242. This creates a subtexture.*

5 Hold a pipe grainer as parallel to the surface as possible, and then draw it down through the glaze. Use a light touch, and work from the top to the bottom. This further softens the glaze and check marks.

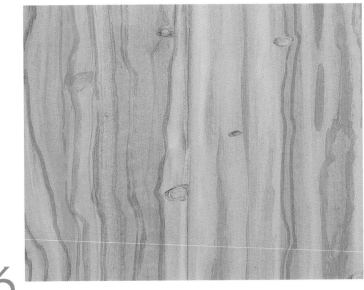

6 Finished knotty pine: the perfect look for a casual or country setting. Seal it with a clear top coat of acrylic varnish or water-based polyurethane.

FORMULA

KNOTTY PINE

SKILL LEVEL: Advanced

RECOMMENDED FOR: Paneled walls; floors; millwork such as flat doors; plain molding; cabinetry; furniture; and accessories

NOT RECOMMENDED FOR: Walls, except when divided into panels, or any surface with intricate carving or elaborate trim

PAIRS OF HANDS NEEDED: 1

TOOLS: Paint buckets; mixing sticks; paint tray; roller with low-nap or foam cover or 3-inch-wide decorator brush; 2 #6 artist's brushes; 90-weight cheesecloth or other soft, lint-free cotton material cut into 6-foot-long pieces and formed into rolls; 3-inch-wide flogging brush; 3-inch-wide pipe grainer; bucket of clean water; clean rags; gloves

BASE COAT: Warm-white eggshell or satin latex paint

GLAZE COLORANT: Universal tints

GLAZE FORMULA: 1 part universal tints and 1 part water

TYPICAL WORKABLE AREA: 2 10- or 12-inch-wide planks

CLEAR TOP COAT: Acrylic varnish or water-based polyurethane

Oak

One of the most heavily and dramatically grained woods, oak requires a careful study of its unique texture before you begin. You'll notice that the dark grain lines seem far apart and that large fibers appear at the pointed part of the heart grain. Use combs to create the grain. Practice beforehand so that you become comfortable with these tools, which require a firm stroke.

Base-coat the surface using an eggshell or satin latex or alkyd enamel, custom-mixed to a color that matches the lightest color in the oak you're reproducing. Let the base coat become thoroughly dry before proceeding.

Masterstroke

Oak has a definite pore structure, which isn't the case with many other woods. In fact, the pores are more distinct than the grain pattern. For another realistic rendering of oak, you may want to use a rolled steel wool pad, which you can drag through the glaze to create prominent "pores." Then apply a fan brush over the glaze to add a subtle grain pattern.

How to Create Oak

1 Mix the glaze to the desired color and thickness. Pour a small amount into the paint tray. Reseal the can.

2 Mask a 12-inch-wide section. Apply glaze, and let it set for a few minutes. Hold a coarse steel graining comb at a 45-degree angle, and rake the surface up and down. Wipe the comb clean, and go over the area several times; then rake it well with a fine graining comb.

3 While the glaze is still wet, make the heart grain and knots by running a graining roller through the glaze in alternate strips, as shown. Work from the top to the bottom, making one pass over each strip. The roller pushes the glaze into the desired grain pattern. If this step leaves too much glaze in the center of the knots, wrap a piece of cheesecloth around your thumb, press it into the center, and wiggle it to remove some of the glaze.

4 Comb the entire surface again with a medium graining comb. Let the comb follow the outline of the heart grain, gradually straightening the line as you move away from the heart grain so that you have straight grain in the middle.

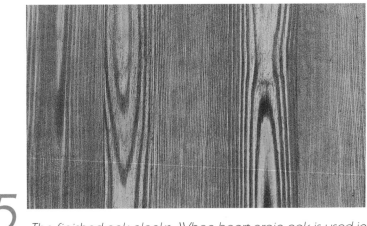

5 The finished oak planks. When heart-grain oak is used in panels, the patterns on adjoining sections always mirror one another. Seal the finish with a clear top coat of satin oil varnish.

F O R M U L A

OAK

SKILL LEVEL: Advanced

RECOMMENDED FOR: Paneled walls; floors; millwork such as flat doors, plain moldings, and paneling; cabinetry; and accessories

NOT RECOMMENDED FOR: Walls, except when divided into panels, or any surface with intricate carving or elaborate trim

PAIRS OF HANDS NEEDED: 1

TOOLS: Painter's masking tape; paper tape; paint buckets; mixing sticks; paint roller with low-nap or foam cover; 3-inch-wide decorator brush; coarse, medium, and fine steel or plastic graining combs; graining roller; clean rags; mineral spirits; gloves

BASE COAT: Custom-mixed eggshell or satin latex or alkyd enamel

GLAZE COLORANT: Universal tints

GLAZE FORMULA: 1 part universal tints, 1 part boiled linseed oil, 2 parts satin oil varnish, and 3 parts mineral spirits

TYPICAL WORKABLE SECTION: 2 10- to 12-inch-wide planks

CLEAR TOP COAT: Satin oil varnish

A Burled Panel

Burled wood is such an easy wood grain to render that it's tempting to use a lot of it. Don't. The wood, which comes from gnarled growth on trees called burls, is rather rare in nature. That means it's expensive and, therefore, seldom used to cover large areas. Follow nature's example, and confine it to small surfaces, such as table tops and cabinet doors. You can also combine it with other wood-grain effects applied to wainscoting, for example. In this case, we've created a burled-wood door panel with a border.

Base-coat the surface with an eggshell or satin latex or alkyd enamel, custom-mixed to a warm, golden wood tone. Let this base coat become thoroughly dry before you proceed.

Masterstroke

Use a thin pointed artist's brush to paint black rings around some of the shapes created by your strokes. This will add authenticity and emphasis to your pattern.

How to Create a Burled Panel

1   *Cut cheesecloth into 6-foot-long pieces, and set them aside. Use painter's masking tape to define the border around the area receiving the burl. Mix universal tints to the desired wood tone, and pour a small amount into a paint tray. Seal the can to keep the solvent from evaporating.*

2   *Coat the entire surface with a thin layer of satin oil varnish taken straight from the can. Ball a piece of cloth in your hand, and moisten it by dipping it into the varnish can. Put just enough varnish on the cloth to make it slide easily on the surface and hold the color in place. Then dip the cloth into the wood-tone color. Work the color over the varnish-coated surface using squiggly circular strokes, as shown.*

3   *Dip a pipe grainer into mineral spirits or turpentine, and off-load the excess on newspaper or paper towels until it's damp, but not wet. Holding it at a 45-degree angle and as parallel to the surface as possible, make short radiating strokes through the burls. Let the burls dry thoroughly.*

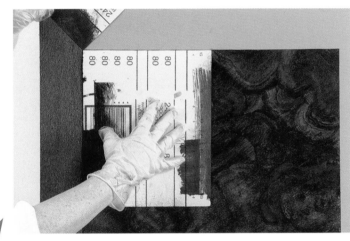

4 For the border, make a glaze with the wood-tone univer-sal tint. Brush it on the border around the burl, using the technique described in "Straight-Grained Mahogany," page 242. Miter the corners of the border by laying 80-grit sandpaper, grit-side down, at a 45-degree angle across each corner, and work the glaze up to and over the miter mask. The sandpaper causes a slight buildup of glaze at these corner joints that highlights the miter.

5 The finished burled panel. It's a fantasy finish that's suit-able for cabinet doors or small wall panels, and it takes on added depth when sealed with a clear top coat of satin oil varnish.

F O R M U L A

A BURLED PANEL

SKILL LEVEL: Intermediate to advanced

RECOMMENDED FOR: Small surfaces like tabletops, accent panels, cabinet doors and drawer fronts, flat doors, and furniture

NOT RECOMMENDED FOR: Walls, unless divided into panels, or any surface with intricate carving or elaborate trim

PAIRS OF HANDS NEEDED: 1

TOOLS: Painter's masking tape; paint buckets; mixing sticks; paint tray; roller with low-nap cover; mixing stick; 3-inch-wide varnish brush; 90-weight cheesecloth cut into 6-foot-long pieces; 3-inch-wide pipe grainer; sheets of 80-grit sandpaper; 3-inch-wide flogging brush; clean rags; mineral spirits; gloves

BASE COAT: Custom-mixed eggshell or satin paint

GLAZE COLORANT: Universal tints

GLAZE FORMULAS: *For burl*—universal tints and satin oil varnish, worked together on the surface. *For straight-grained borders*—1 part universal tints, 1 part boiled linseed oil, 2 parts satin oil varnish, and 3 parts mineral spirits

TYPICAL WORKABLE SECTION: A 2- to 3-square-foot area or surface

CLEAR TOP COAT: Satin oil varnish

Bibliography

Constantine, Albert, Jr. *Know Your Woods.* Revised by Harry J. Hobbs. New York: Charles Scribner's Sons, 1975.

Corbella, Enrico. *The Architect's Handbook of Marble, Granite and Stone.* 3 vols. New York: Van Nostrand Reinhold, 1990.

Fleming, John, and Hugh Honour. *Dictionary of Decorative Arts.* New York: Harper & Row, 1977.

Gamblin, Robert, and Martha Bergman-Gamblin. *Gamblin Color Book.* Portland, OR: Gamblin Artists Colors, 1996.

The Home Decorating Institute. *Painted Illusions.* Minnetonka, MN: Cy DeCosse, 1996.

Innes, Jocasta. *Decorating with Paint.* New York: Harmony Books, 1986.

————. *The New Paint Magic.* New York: Pantheon Books, 1992.

Marx, Ina Brosseau, Allen Marx, and Robert Marx. *Professional Painted Finishes.* New York: Watson-Guptill Publications, 1991.

Mayer, Ralph. *The Artist's Handbook of Materials and Techniques.* Revised by Steven Sheehan. New York: Viking, Penguin, 1991.

McCloud, Kevin. *Kevin McCloud's Complete Book of Paint and Decorative Techniques.* New York: Simon & Schuster, 1996.

Munsell, Albert H. *A Color Notion: An Illustrated System Defining All Color and Their Relations by Measured Scale of Their Hue, Value and Chroma.* Baltimore: Munsell Color (Macbeth), 1988.

O'Neill, Isabel. *The Art of the Painted Finish for Furniture and Decoration.* New York: William Morrow & Company, 1971.

Sloan, Annie, and Kate Gwynn. *The Complete Book of Decorative Painting Techniques.* Topsfield, MA: Salem House Publishers, 1988.

Stott, Rowena, and Jane Cheshire. *The Country Diary Book of Stencilling.* New York: Viking, 1988.

Victorian Stencils: Design and Decoration. Dover Pictorial Archives Series. Mineola, NY: Dover Publications, 1968

Sources — Supplies and Tools

Albert Constantine & Son, Inc.
2050 Eastchester Road
Bronx, NY 10461
(800) 223-8087
Retail store and mail order. Paint strippers, varnishes, and brushes

Art Essentials of New York Ltd.
3 Cross Street
Suffern, NY 10901-4601
(914) 368-1100
(800) 283-5323 for retail stores carrying their products
Distributor of gold-leaf supplies and books on gilding

Art Supply Warehouse
5325 Departure Drive
Raleigh, NC 27616
(800) 995-6778
Artist materials. Free catalog

Binney and Smith Inc.
1100 Church Lane
P.O. Box 431
Easton, PA 18044-0431
(610) 253-6271 in PA
(800) 272-9652 outside PA
Publishers of Liquitex Color Maps and Mixing Guides

Dick Blick Fine Art Co.
P.O. Box 1267
Galesburg, IL 61402
(309) 343-6181
(800) 447-8192 for mail orders
Retail stores in the Midwest and mail order. Paints, brushes, and general art supplies

Dixie Art Supplies
2612 Jefferson Highway
New Orleans, LA 70121
(800) 783-2612
Artist materials. Free catalog

Eagle Supply Company
327 West 42nd Street
New York, NY 10036
(212) 246-6180
Sign painters' supplies. Mail order via UPS C.O.D.

The Easel Connection
2820 Sunset Lane #95
Henderson, KY 42420
(800) 916-2278
Artist materials. Free catalog

Finesse Pinstriping Inc.
P.O. Box 54128 Linden Hill Station
Flushing, NY 11354

(800) 228-1258
Manufacturer of pinstriping tape. Call for location of nearest distributor

Sam Flax, Inc.
12 West 20th Street
New York, NY 10011
(800) 628-9512
Retail and mail order. General art and graphic art supplies

Gail Grisi Stenciling, Inc.
P.O. Box 1263
Haddonfield, NJ 08033
(609) 354-1757 in NJ
(800) 338-1325 outside NJ
Retail stores in NJ and mail order. Precut stencils and paint

The Italian Art Store
84 Maple Avenue
Morristown, NJ 07960
(800) 643-6440
Artist materials. Free catalog

Lab Safety Supply, Inc.
P.O. Box 1368
Janesville, WI 53547-1368
Manufacturer and distributor of safety clothing and equipment

Lee Valley Tools
1090 Morrison Drive
Ottawa, Ontario K2H 1C2
Canada
(613) 596-0350
Mail order available. Brushes,
paints, and glazes

Lee's Art Shop Inc.
220 West 57th Street
New York, NY 10019
(212) 247-0110
Retail and mail order. General
art supplies, including sea
sponges and color-mixing guides

Leo Uhlfelder Co.
420 South Fulton Avenue
Mount Vernon, NY 10553
(914) 664-8701
Importer and manufacturer of
gold leaf and brushes

Liberty Paints
Routes 66 and 23B
Hudson, NY 12534
(518) 828-4060
Retail and mail order. Wide
range of products, including
paints, glazes, and brushes

New York Central Art Supply
62 Third Avenue
New York, NY 10003

(212) 473-7705 (store)
(212) 477-0400 for mail order
in NY
(800) 950-6111 for mail order
outside NY
Retail and mail order general art
supplies, including specialty
brushes

Pearl Paint Co., Inc.
308 Canal Street
New York, NY 10013
(212) 431-7932 in NY
(800) 221-6845 outside NY
Retail and mail order. House
and artists' paints, wide range of
brushes, safety equipment, sea
sponges, color-mixing charts,
steel combs, other general art
supplies

Seaway Artist Supplies
135 Broadway
Marine City, MI 48039
(800) 968-1862
Artist supplies. Free catalog

Sepp Leaf Products Inc.
381 Park Avenue South,
Suite 1301
New York, NY 10016
(212) 683-2840 in NY
(800) 971-7377 outside NY
Mail-order gold-leaf supplies

T. J. Ronan Paint Corp.
749 East 135th Street
Bronx, NY 10454
(718) 292-1100 in NY
(800) 24-RONAN outside NY
Manufacturer of Japan colors

Utrecht Manufacturing Corp.
33 35th Street
Brooklyn, NY 11232
(718) 768-2525
(800) 223-9132 for mail order
Retail stores in New York, Detroit,
Chicago, Philadelphia, Boston,
Washington, DC, Berkeley,
Seattle, San Francisco, and Los
Angeles. General art supplies

Winsor & Newton, Inc.
11 Constitution Avenue
Piscataway, NJ 08855
(973) 562-0770
Distributor of artists' paints and
brushes. Call to find nearest retail
store carrying their products

Woodcrafters Lumber Sales Inc.
212 Northeast Sixth Avenue
Portland, OR 97232
(800) 777-3709
Retail and mail order paint
strippers, varnishes, shellacs, sea
sponges, specialty moldings, and
architectural elements

The Woodworker's Store

4365 Willow Drive

Medina, MN 55340

(612) 478-8200 in MN

(800) 279-4441 outside MN

Twenty retail stores nationwide
and mail order. Paint strippers,
brushes, varnishes, and wood
fillers

**Woodworker's Supply of
New Mexico**

5604 Alameda Place Northeast

Albuquerque, NM 87113

(800) 645-9292

Retail and mail-order. Paint
strippers, varnishes, and wood
fillers

Sources — House Paint, Glaze, and Varnish Manufacturers

Absolute Coatings Inc.

38 Portman Road

New Rochelle, NY 10801

(914) 636-0822 in NY

(800) 221-8010 outside NY

Varnishes available nationwide

Benjamin Moore & Co.

51 Chestnut Ridge Road

Montvale, NJ 07645

(800) 344-0400

Products available nationwide

The Glidden Co.

925 Euclid Avenue

Cleveland, OH 44115

(216) 344-8800 in OH

(800) 221-4100 outside OH

Products available nationwide

Martin-Senour Paints

101 Prospect Avenue

Cleveland, OH 44115

(800) 542-8468

Products available nationwide
through dealers

McCloskey Varnish Co.

1191 Wheeling Road

Wheeling, IL 60090

(800) 345-4530

Ready-mixed glazes and
varnishes available through
dealers

Pratt & Lambert, Inc.

P.O. Box 22

Buffalo, NY 14240

(718) 873-6000

Paints, ready-mixed glazes, and
varnishes available nationwide

Samuel Cabot Inc.

100 Hale Street

Newburyport, MA 01950

(978) 465-1900 in MA

(800) US-STAIN outside MA

Products available nationwide

Sherwin-Williams

101 Prospect Avenue

Cleveland, OH 44115

(800) 474-3794

Products available nationwide
through Sherwin-Williams stores

Glossary

Acetate. The plastic sheet material used for cutting stencils.

Acrylic. A water-based plastic polymer that acts as the binder in acrylic paints.

Acrylic varnish. A coating that contains the same medium used to make water-soluble paints and glazes.

Advancing colors. The warm colors. As with dark colors, they seem to advance toward you.

Alizarin crimson. One of the basic pigments, alizarin crimson is synthetically derived from coal tar and ranges from scarlet to maroon.

Alkyd paints. Paints with artificial resins (alkyds) forming their binder; often imprecisely called "oil-based" paints. Alkyds have replaced the linseed oil formerly used as a binder in oil-based paint.

Analogous colors. Any three colors located next to one another on the color wheel.

Antiquing. Any technique used to make a painted surface look old; usually refers to a thin glaze that is applied to a surface, allowing the undercoat to show through.

Artist's acrylics. Paints that contain pigments suspended in acrylic resin, similar to latex paint but of much higher quality.

Artist's oils. The tube or oil-stick paint associated with fine-art paintings. They consist of pigments suspended in linseed oil, and come in a wide range of saturated colors.

Binder. A viscous, pliant material that holds pigments in suspension and makes them adhere to surfaces—the bulk of what makes up paint.

Blender brushes. Specialty brushes used to blend and soften all types of wet surfaces.

Boxing. Pouring all paint of the same color and formula into one large container and then mixing it together to eliminate minor variations in color between cans.

Breccia marble. Marble that is composed of sharp fragments cemented together. ▲

Burled wood. Wood that has been cut from a gnarled, knotty part of a tree, giving it a curved and irregular grain pattern. ▲

Burnt sienna. One of the native colors, this is a deep, rich rust-red made from calcined raw sienna.

Burnt umber. One of the native colors, burnt umber is a dark reddish brown made from calcined raw umber.

Cadmium orange. One of the basic pigments, cadmium orange is made from cadmium sulphide and cadmium selenide.

Casein paint. An old-fashioned paint made by mixing pigments with milk solids. It is seldom used today except on furniture where a faded look is desired.

Cheesecloth. A loosely woven cotton gauze used to create many different textures as well as to blend and smooth all techniques.

Cheesecloth distressing. The process of blending and softening paint strokes and colors by pouncing bunched-up cheesecloth over the wet surface. ▼

China bristles. Another term for bristles made from boar hair.

Chroma. *See* Intensity.

Chrome green. A variety of green pigments made from chrome yellow and iron (Prussian) blue.

Chrome orange. One of the basic pigments, this orange-red pigment is made from lead chromate and lead oxides.

Chrome yellow. One of the basic pigments, this yellow pigment is made from lead chromate combined with lead sulfate.

Clear top coat. A transparent finishing layer of protection applied on top of a painted finish.

Color scheme. A group of colors used together to create visual harmony in a space.

Color washing. Random layers of thin glaze that are blended to produce a faded, uneven look similar to that of whitewash or distemper. ◤

Color wheel. A pie-shaped diagram showing the range and relationships of pigment. The three primary colors are equidistant, with secondary and tertiary colors in between them.

Combing. Any paint technique that involves marking narrow lines of color on a surface. Also called *strié* or *dragging*. Combing techniques that specifically intend to imitate wood are called wood-graining techniques.

Complementary colors. Colors located opposite one another on the color wheel.

Contrast. The art of assembling colors with different values and intensities to create visual harmony in a color scheme.

Cool colors. The greens, blues, and violets.

Cutters. Short, stiff-bristled brushes used to cut in lines, such as in corners and around trim.

Deglossing. Roughing up a surface before painting so that it has "tooth," a texture that grabs paint.

Distemper. An old-fashioned type of interior paint made with a casein or gelatin/glue size binder.

Double-split complementaries. Colors on either side of two complementary colors on the color wheel.

Dragging. *See* Combing

Dusting brushes. Soft, medium-length brushes used for combing, stippling, and softening textures.

Earth tones. The natural colors of earth; browns and beiges.

Eggshell. A thin, brittle semi-matte paint finish.

Enamel. Paint with finely ground pigments and a high binder content so that it dries to a hard gloss or semigloss finish.

Faux. French for "false"—used to describe any technique in which paint imitates another substance, such as wood or stone.

Ferrule. The metal part of a paintbrush that holds the bristles to the handle.

Flags. A word describing bristles with split ends, which help hold the paint.

Flogging brush. Wide, long-bristled brushes used to texture surfaces by dragging or slapping wet paint or glaze. Also called draggers.

Glaze. A paint or colorant mixed with a transparent medium and diluted with a thinner compatible with the medium.

Gloss. A shiny finish that reflects the maximum amount of light.

Graining combs. Flexible steel or plastic combs that come in a variety of sizes and are used to striate and grain surfaces.

Heart grain. Wood with a V-shaped grain pattern. ▶

Hue. Synonym for color. Used most often to describe the color family to which a color belongs.

Intensity. The brightness or dullness of a color. Also referred to as a color's purity or saturation.

Intermediate colors. Colors made by mixing equal amounts of one primary and one secondary color, such as red-orange and blue-green.

Japan colors. Concentrated oil-based colorants that are used for tinting alkyd paints and solvent-soluble glazes. Japan colors have an intense, flat color and will dry quickly.

Jasper. An opaque form of quartz that is usually yellow, brown, red, or green. ▼

Lampblack. One of the native colors, lampblack is a deep black made from nearly pure carbon (containing some oil and tar impurities).

Latex paints. Paints that contain acrylic or vinyl resins or a combination of the two. High-quality latex paints contain 100 percent acrylic resin. Latex paints are water-soluble; that is, they can be thinned and cleaned up with water.

Leveling. The ability of a paint to smooth out after application so that it shows no brush or roller marks when dry.

Lining brushes. Thin, flexible, long-bristled brushes used for fine lining and detail work.

Linseed oil. An oil derived from flax seed used in oil-based paints and varnishes.

Mineral spirits. A petroleum distillate used as a solvent for alkyd-based paint.

Morocco leather. A soft and expensive leather made from the skin of goat tanned with sumac; by extension, a paint technique imitating it. ◄

Mottler. A flat-ended brush used to make textures in glazed surfaces.

Mylar. A trademarked name for a strong but thin polyester film, often with a metallic pigmentation.

Nap. A soft or fuzzy surface on fabric (such as a paint roller cover).

Native colors. The basic inorganic pigments derived from pigmented earth colored by minerals, and used to make the basic colors found in artist's oil paints: burnt sienna, burnt umber, lamp-black, raw sienna, raw umber, and yellow ochre.

Negative technique. Any decorative painting technique that involves removing paint from a surface while it is still wet. *See also* Positive technique.

Oil varnish. *See* Varnish.

Overglaze. A thin glaze added as a final step to a decorative finish. It can be the original glaze thinned somewhat or a new, thinner glaze in another color.

Overgrainers. Long, flat-bristled brushes used to apply paint detail, generally on dry, previously grained surfaces.

Palette knife. An artist's knife with a dull, flexible blade, used for mixing paints on a palette.

Parchment. An animal skin used for writing, or paper made in imitation of it; by extension, the decorative finish that has a similar appearance. ▼

Pastel. A color to which a lot of white has been added to make it very light in value.

Pigment. The substances that give paint color. Pigments are derived from natural or synthetic materials that have been ground into fine powders.

Polyurethane. A plastic resin, which makes a good top coat for most types of paint except artist's oils. Thin it with mineral spirits, or with water if water-based polyurethane.

Positive technique. Any painting technique that involves adding paint to a surface. *See also* Negative technique.

Primary colors. Red, yellow, and blue; the three colors in the visible spectrum that cannot be broken down into other colors. In various combinations and proportions, they make all other colors.

Primer. A coating that prepares surfaces for painting by making them more uniform in texture and giving them tooth.

Quaternary colors. Colors made by mixing two tertiary colors.

Ragging off. The technique in which paint is pulled from a surface using a bunched-up cloth. Sometimes called "cheese-clothing." ◄

Ragging on. The technique in which paint is applied to a surface using a bunched-up cloth. ◄

Rag-rolling off. A technique in which paint or glaze is removed from a surface using a rolled-up piece of cloth that is lifted off in a rhythmic pattern.

Raw sienna. One of the native colors, raw sienna is an earthy yellow-brown made from clay containing iron and aluminum oxides, which is found in the area of Tuscany around Siena.

Raw umber. One of the native colors, raw umber is a cool brown made from a clay containing iron oxides and manganese dioxide, originally from the Italian region of Umbria.

Receding colors. The cool colors. They make surfaces seem farther from the eye.

Red ochre. One of the basic pigments, red ochre is a red tinged slightly with violet, made from clay containing iron oxide.

Refined white beeswax. Derived from natural beeswax, this product produces an elegant, lustrous finish that doesn't yellow.

Registration marks. Small holes cut into a stencil with more than one layer, which allow you to match up the different layers.

Resin. A category of solid or semisolid, viscous substances, both natural (rosin, amber, copal) and synthetic (polyvinyl, polystyrene).

Round fitches. Round brushes with firm but flexible bristles. They are used for spattering, stippling, and stenciling.

Rust inhibitors. Chemicals added to special paints intended for metal surfaces that may corrode.

Sealer. A product (for example, shellac) that seals porous surfaces by forming a durable, non-absorbent barrier that prevents them from sucking up paint.

Sea sponge. The fibrous connective structure of a sea creature, used to apply and remove paint. Not to be confused with the cellulose variety used in household chores.

Secondary colors. Orange, green, and violet; the colors made by mixing equal amounts of two primary colors.

Semigloss. A slightly lustrous finish that is light reflective and has an appearance somewhere between gloss and eggshell.

Shade. A color to which black has been added to make it darker.

Sheen. The quality of paint that reflects light.

Shellac. The secretion of a Southeast Asian insect dissolved in alcohol, which is used as a sealer. It comes in three colors: *clear* (sometimes labeled "white"); *white-pigmented* (also referred to as *opaque* and *chalked white*), and *orange,* or *blond.*

Snap time. The point at which a paint or glaze has begun to dull down and become tacky. After snap time, a paint cannot be worked without causing damage to the finish.

Solvent. A liquid capable of dissolving another substance (such as mineral spirits for alkyd paint and water for latex paint).

Spalter. A type of natural-bristle brush used for smoothing on alkyd paints.

Spattering. The technique of applying random dots of paint over a surface by striking a saturated brush or rubbing paint through a screen. ◄

Split complementary. A color paired with the colors on either side of its complementary color on the color wheel.

Sponging. A paint technique that uses a natural sea sponge to put paint on or take paint off a surface. ▼

Stencil. A cut-out pattern that allows you to paint the same motif over and over. Complex stencils will have several overlapping patterns, and different colors are applied in layers after the previous coat dries.

Stippling. A paint technique that involves pouncing a special brush straight up and down over a surface, creating myriad tiny dots that blend together when viewed from a distance. Similar to the fine-art technique known as pointillism. ▼

Stippling brush. A blocky, stiff-bristled china brush used to stipple wet paints, glazes, and top coats.

Strié. *See* Combing.

Tempera paint. A mixture of pigments and a water-soluble glutinous emulsion binder, often made from an oil extracted from egg yolks.

Terebene dryer. A substance (prepared from oil of turpentine) that can be added to alkyd-based paints (most often house paints) to speed their drying.

Tertiary colors. Colors made by combining equal amounts of two secondary colors.

Texturing compounds. Substances that go into paints where a rough, grained, or dimensional quality is desired.

Thinner. A liquid that is mixed with paint to make it less thick, such as turpentine or white mineral spirits for alkyd-based paints and water for latex-based paints.

Tint. A color to which white has been added to make it lighter in value.

Titanium white. The most common white pigment, titanium white is a brilliant white that is synthetically derived from the metal titanium.

Tone. A color to which gray has been added to change its value.

Tooth. The coarse quality of a surface (or a coating on a surface) that improves the performance, appearance, and longevity of paint.

Triad. Any three colors located equidistant from one another on the color wheel.

Trompe l'oeil. French for "fool the eye"—used to describe a painted surface that convincingly mimics reality (such as the painted sky in the picture below). ▼

Turpentine. A solvent made from distillate of pine resins, used as a thinner and cleaner for alkyd-based paints.

Ultramarine blue. One of the native colors, ultramarine blue is an intense blue originally made from crushed lapis lazuli, but now formulated from man-made pigments.

Universal tints. Pigments that are combined with ethylene glycol and a small amount of water. They are usable in both water- and alkyd-based paints and glaze mediums.

Value. The lightness (tint or pastel) and darkness (shade) of a color.

Value scale. A graphic tool used to show the range of values between pure white and true black.

Varnish. The traditional top coat used in decorative painting, consisting of an oil-based paint with a solvent and an oxidizing or evaporating binder, which leaves behind a thin, hard film.

Vehicle. *See* Binder.

Vermillion red. One of the basic pigments, vermilion red is a brilliant pure red made from mercuric sulphide.

Visible spectrum. The bands of hues created when sunlight passes through a prism.

Warm colors. Generally, the reds, oranges, and yellows; often including the browns.

Wash. A thinned-out latex or acrylic paint. ◄

Water-based polyurethane. A sealer made from polyurethane resins that is water- rather than oil-soluble.

Wavelength. The means of measuring the electromagnetic spectrum; the portion of this spectrum that is visible to us as light has waves that measure between 4,000 and 7,000 angstroms, with red having the longest waves and violet the shortest.

Wet edge. A margin of wet paint or glaze. Leaving a wet edge creates a seamless blend between sections.

Wood graining. A painting technique that seeks to resemble wood by imitating the lines found in cut lumber (which are the tree's growth rings). ◄

Wood stain. A translucent combination of solvent (either water- or alkyd-based) and pigment, usually in colors imitating natural wood, which allow some of the wood's natural color and its grain to show through.

Yellow ochre. One of the native colors, yellow ochre is a mustard-yellow made from clay containing iron oxide.

Zinc white. A common white pigment, zinc white is a brilliant white synthetically derived from the metal zinc.

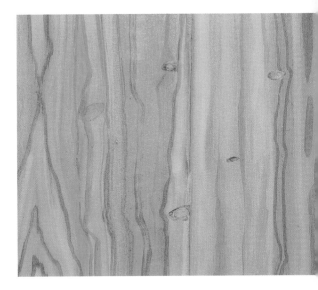

Index

Have a home decorating, improvement, or gardening project? Look for these and other fine Creative Homeowner books wherever books are sold.

Design advice and industry tips for choosing window treatments. Over 225 illustrations. 176pp., 9"×10"
BOOK #: 279431

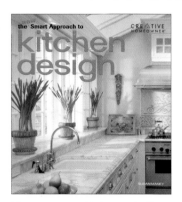

How to create kitchen style like a pro. Over 260 color photographs. 208 pp.; 9"×10"
BOOK #: 279946

How to work with space, color, pattern, texture. Over 400 photos. 288 pp.; 9"×10"
BOOK #: 279672

All you need to know about designing a bath. Over 260 color photos. 208 pp., 9"×10"
BOOK #: 279234

Original ideas for decorating and organizing kids' rooms. Over 200 illustrations. 176 pp., 9"×10"
BOOK#: 279473

Projects to personalize your rooms with paint and paper. 300 color photos. 176 pp.; 9"×10"
BOOK#: 279723

Learn how to make the most of color. More than 150 color photos. 176 pp.; 9"×10"
BOOK #: 287264

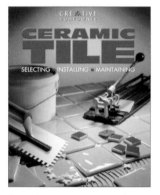

Everything you need to know about setting ceramic tile. Over 450 photos. 160 pp.; 8½"×10⅞"
BOOK#: 277524

Complete houseplant guide. 200 readily available plants; more than 400 photos. 192 pp.; 9"×10"
BOOK #: 275243

An impressive guide to garden design and plant selection. More than 600 color photos. 320 pp.; 9"×10"
BOOK#: 274615

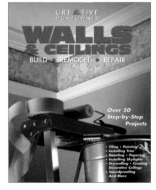

How to replace old surfaces with new ones. Over 450 illustrations. 160 pp.; 8½"×10⅞"
BOOK#: 277708

The ultimate home improvement reference manual. over 300 step-by-step projects. 608 pp.; 9"×10⅞"
BOOK#: 267855